Suicide
Prohibition

Suicide

THE SHAME OF MEDICINE

Prohibition

Thomas Szasz

SYRACUSE UNIVERSITY PRESS

∞ The paper used in this publication meets the minimum requirements
of the American National Standard for Information Sciences—Permanence
of Paper for Printed Library Materials, ANSI Z39.48-1992.

For a listing of books published and distributed by Syracuse University Press,
visit our Web site at SyracuseUniversityPress.syr.edu.

ISBN: 978-0-8156-0990-2

Library of Congress Cataloging-in-Publication Data

Szasz, Thomas Stephen, 1920–
    Suicide prohibition : the shame of medicine / Thomas Szasz. — 1st ed.
        p. ; cm.
    Includes bibliographical references and index.
    ISBN 978-0-8156-0990-2 (cloth : alk. paper)
    I. Title.
    [DNLM: 1. Suicide—prevention & control—United States.   2. Suicide—
psychology—United States.   3. Health Policy—United States.   4. Personal
Autonomy—United States.   5. Suicide—ethics—United States. WM 165]
    LC-classification not assigned
    616.85'8445—dc23   2011032776

Manufactured in the United States of America

Nothing is so firmly believed as what is least known.

—MICHEL DE MONTAIGNE (1533–92)

THOMAS SZASZ is a Professor Emeritus of Psychiatry at the State University of New York Upstate Medical University in Syracuse. The author of more than six hundred articles and thirty-three books, he is widely recognized as the leading critic of the coercive interventions employed by the psychiatric establishment.

Contents

PREFACE • *ix*

ACKNOWLEDGMENTS • *xv*

Introduction • *1*

1. Suicide Prohibition • *13*

2. The Suicide Prohibition Agent • *46*

3. The Marriage of Asclepius and Atropos • *66*

4. Separation: *Emigration, Secession, Suicide* • *75*

5. The Shame of Medicine • *95*

6. Envoi • *104*

APPENDIX: *"On Suicide" by David Hume* • *109*

NOTES • *113*

BIBLIOGRAPHY • *123*

INDEX • *129*

Preface

FOR THE PERSON WHO TAKES HIS OWN LIFE, suicide is, prima facie, a solution. Nevertheless, we think, and are enjoined to think, that suicide is a problem, specifically a mental health or psychiatric problem. This is a novel idea and a very odd one. The idea of "suicide prevention" is odder still.

Suicide is legal, but failed suicide is not: it is a violation of mental health laws, punished by coercions called "hospitalization" and "treatment."

Suicide is legal, but assisted suicide is not: it is a violation of the criminal laws, punished by criminal sanctions, unless the "assistance" is rendered by a physician and is explicitly authorized by law, in which case it is considered a medical treatment called "physician-assisted suicide" (PAS).

Suicide is legal, but is penalized and stigmatized in novel ways: if the act is committed by an active member of the armed forces, White House policy enjoins "the President from sending a letter of condolence to family members of troops who die by suicide"; and if the person who kills himself is receiving so-called mental health treatment, his therapist is likely to be accused of malpractice and declared guilty of it.[1]

What do we mean when we say that an act is legal? We mean that the actor is free to speak about, plan, and perform it without penalty by agents of the state. Discussing and planning, say, cooking, or trying to cook and making a mess of it, are matters of indifference to the law. However, discussing and planning to kill oneself, or trying to do so and failing, are psychiatric transgressions, violations of mental health laws. Categorized as "dangerousness to self or others," these acts are punished by deprivations of liberty and coercions, called "hospitalization" and "treatment."

Finally, so-called assisted suicide is a criminal offense— unless the assistance is provided by a licensed physician in a jurisdiction in which specific legislation explicitly permits it: then it is a medical service. If doctors performed assisted suicide by shooting, stabbing, or strangling us, at our request, would we still call it "physician-assisted suicide"? Would we still classify and condone it as a medical treatment?

The truth is that the only thing that makes physician-assisted suicide a medical service is that the means used for it is a prescription for a barbiturate. Socrates, let us recall, died of assisted suicide: he killed himself by ingesting a lethal dose of a substance the Greeks called *pharmakon*—a word that means both medicine and poison—procured for him by others. The Greeks did not need medical help to kill themselves. Why do we act as if we do? Because we like the idea of dying peacefully, with a drug that puts us to sleep—forever—and because, at the same time, we wage wars on drugs especially useful for this purpose and suborn physicians to bootleg them. In the absence of prescription laws—and, more generally, of drug prohibition—there would be no need for, and no special problem of, physician-assisted suicide.

If suicide be deemed a problem, it is a moral and political problem. Managing it as if it were a medical problem will succeed only in debasing medicine and corrupting the law. Although the air we breathe is heavily polluted with antisuicide propaganda, it cannot extinguish the knowledge that, at bottom, suicide is a solution. Authoritatively repressed, such knowledge reemerges as humor: "I was depressed last night so I called Lifeline. . . . Got a freakin' call center in Pakistan. I told them I was suicidal. . . . They got all excited and asked if I could drive a truck."[2]

Two hundred years ago, Johann Wolfgang von Goethe (1749–1832) observed, "Suicide is an event that is a part of human nature."[3] If suicide is a part of human nature, why do physicians, especially psychiatrists, regard thinking about it as "suicidal ideation," a symptom of mental illness or side effect of one or another "medication," and wage war against voluntary death as a deadly enemy? In this book I try to answer this question by turning our customary inquiry around, focusing on the agents of suicide prevention-prohibition who eagerly stigmatize individuals who foolishly share their private thoughts with them, instead of their stigmatized victims, persons the professionals deem "dangerous to themselves."

The notion that we own ourselves, hence have a "right" to end our lives, is a modern idea. It was first fully articulated by the Scottish philosopher David Hume (1711–76), in his posthumously published essay "On Suicide": "Has not every one . . . the free disposal of his own life? And may he not lawfully employ that power with which nature has endowed him?"[4]

The traditional notion, that we belong to our Creator or to our community, was restated, with a psychiatric gloss, by Benjamin Rush (1745–1813), the founding father of American psychiatry. He declared, "Every man possesses an absolute power over his own liberty and property, but not over his own life. . . . [H]e has no right to dispose of his life. . . . Suicide is madness."[5]

If suicide is madness, and if madness is a condition that deprives the madman of his free will (in legal terms, guilty mind, mens rea), then suicide ceases to be self-murder. Instead, pondering ending one's life becomes "suicidality," the symptom of an illness, and suicide becomes the consequence of an "untreated" illness. Enter the psychiatrist as an indispensable player in this drama: his role is to protect the individual from "dangerousness to himself" by depriving him of liberty. Every "involuntary treatment act" in every state makes "danger to self" an act punishable by civil commitment. Thus has the prohibition of suicide—typically called "suicide prevention"—become a vast, bureaucratic legal-psychiatric enterprise. From the politician's and psychiatrist's point of view, it is lifesaving medical treatment. From the subject's point of view, it is illegal and unjustified imprisonment:

> I am a doctoral student in psychology. Several months ago I was involuntarily committed to a psychiatric ward in a general hospital. I was depressed and, seeking support, had called my parents and told them that I was suicidal. They promptly called the police, who arrived at my apartment, handcuffed me, and transported me to the local psychiatric center. There I was placed in a lobby with several psychotic patients. I remained there for 5 hours before I was evaluated by a psychiatrist. She spoke to me for approximately 10 minutes before she decided that it was in my "best interest" for me to be committed to a psychiatric ward. I protested, of course, believing that wrenching me away from life would cause far more harm than good. She expressed no empathy, however, and sent me back to the lobby. I remained there for 12 more hours, during which time she passed by me numerous times without bothering to make eye contact.—After being transferred to the hospital ward, I was placed in a room with an actively psychotic woman. I remained there for the weekend, during which time not a single hospital employee asked me why I was depressed. I was offered Celexa [a so-called antidepressant] and took it only when a nurse suggested that my refusal to take medication might be perceived as "resistant" and thus delay my discharge. The Celexa made me so ill that I could hardly get out of bed; although the ward psychiatrist was aware of my reaction to the medication, he did not consider changing the drug or the dosage. On Monday morning, I met with the ward psychiatrist, who told me that I would have to remain in the hospital. I asked her how she had come

to that conclusion, given that she hadn't spoken to me once since my arrival at the hospital. She replied, "I have experience." She went on to tell me that I had a "control problem" and that I refused to relinquish control to the hospital staff. I was stunned. I had never before thought that a goal of psychiatric care was to rob the patient of control. Apparently patients who ask questions are considered insolent. I was finally released from the hospital five days after my arrival. I can certainly say that I received no benefit from my stay in the psychiatric ward. I am more depressed than I was before, having been traumatized by my experience with the mental health care system.[6]

Laws that enable some persons to lock up some other persons whose behavior they find upsetting have nothing to do with health, medicine, or treatment: they are a system of extralegal social controls without the due-process safeguards of the criminal justice system. Calling the arrangement "suicide prevention" is deception and self-deception. The noncoercive prevention of death may, depending on circumstances, be a noble end.[7] The coercive prohibition of it is, a priori, ignoble and unworthy of modern people in secular societies.[8]

Acknowledgments

I OWE A VERY SPECIAL DEBT to Anthony Stadlen for his generous and invaluable assistance. I thank also Mira de Vries; Keith Hoeller; Roger Yanow; my son-in-law, Steve Peters; and my brother, George, for reading the manuscript and their helpful suggestions; and, as always, the staff of the Library of the Upstate Medical University of the State University of New York in Syracuse for their unstinting help.

Suicide
Prohibition

Introduction

1

Birth and death are biological events, the consequences of ante-
cedent actions or occurrences. In the animal world, both events
are pure happenings, outside the scope of the organism's understanding or influence. The development of human consciousness
and intelligence creates conditions that enable humans to bring
these events under their partial or even complete control, depending on their understanding of the biological processes involved,
their moral-religious attitudes toward exercising such controls,
and their willingness or unwillingness to assume personal
responsibility for doing so.

   Birth control is a familiar term and common practice, prohibited or permitted, discouraged or encouraged, by governments,
depending on their religious beliefs and economic-ideological
interests. Death control is analogous to birth control. Nevertheless, the term is unfamiliar. If implemented by the government—
in war or execution for crime—the practice is considered a matter
of morality, law, and politics, not medicine. If implemented by the
individual on himself—in suicide—the practice, as I showed in
the preface, is widely regarded as a matter of medicine, a mental
illness treated by deprivation of liberty and coerced drugging.[1]
Moreover, as I note later, in the United States judicial killing
(execution by injection) is medicalized, and in National Socialist

1

Germany, so was practically all state-sponsored murder, including the Holocaust.

Let us not forget Robert Servatius's defense of his client Adolf Eichmann in his trial in Jerusalem: "It [killing by gas] was indeed a medical matter, since it was prepared by physicians; it was a matter of killing, and killing, too, is a medical matter."[2]

The medicalization of judicial killing may be said to have begun with the guillotine, making execution ostensibly painless. It led to execution by a kind of debauched general anesthesia, first by the inhalation of a lethal gas, then by the intravenous injection of lethal drugs. Self-killing proved to be even better suited for medicalization. After the Second World War, medical control of the suicidal person—called "suicide prevention"—became an important part of the profession of psychiatry. The formal medicalization of physician-permitted or physician-provided voluntary death—called "physician-assisted suicide"—soon followed. Typically, PAS is simply the semilegal bootlegging of barbiturates by doctors. Medical ethicists and civil libertarians view it as progress in patient autonomy. I see it as just the opposite.[3]

Death is an unavoidable event: its occurrence is not in our hands, but its timing may be, if we so choose. Because we approve of birth control, we do not reflexively attribute mental illness to its practitioner, do not impugn his competence to engage in the practice, and do not engage in "contraception prevention" to protect him from harming himself. In contrast, we disapprove of suicide, reflexively attribute mental illness to its practitioner, impugn his competence to engage in the practice, and engage in "suicide prevention" to protect him from harming himself.

Although the deleterious economic and social consequences of irresponsible procreation are demonstrably greater than the deleterious consequences of irresponsible suicide, we treat the opportunity to procreate, but not the opportunity to practice death control, as if it were an inalienable right. We regard the coercive regulation of personal birth control as morally odious and legally impermissible. I believe we ought to regard the coercive regulation of personal death control similarly.

The Bible writers wisely reminded us that life is a cycle of birth, growth, decline, and death: "To every thing there is a season, and a time to every purpose under the heaven: A time to be born, and a time to die" (Eccles. 3:2). There comes a time when a woman is too old to have a child. If she does not want to end up childless, she must have a baby while she can, perhaps earlier than she might feel ready for the task. Unless we die in a timely fashion, there comes a moment after which we are unable to kill ourselves. If we do not want to die a lingering death after a protracted period of pathetic disability, we must kill ourselves while we can, perhaps earlier than we might feel ready to do so.

2

We are not responsible for being born. But from the moment we acquire the power of self-reflection, we are, increasingly as we age, responsible for how we live and how we die. The option of killing oneself is intrinsic to human existence (except during early childhood and sometimes in old age).

We are born involuntarily. Religion, psychiatry, and the state insist that we die the same way. Reason tells us that we have just as much right and responsibility to regulate how we die as how we live. To be sure, suicidal activity, like any intimate bodily personal activity, ought to be permissible only in private. Public displays of self-harm or of the intention to kill oneself—exemplified by a person's threatening to jump from a high building—are an interference with the everyday activities of others and a violation of their rights. They ought to be prohibited and punished by the criminal law.

Most people today, perhaps everyone in the secular West, believe that they "own" their bodies and lives. When people are killed by others, we say they have been deprived of their right to life. But when they kill themselves, we do not say they have exercised their right to self-ownership. Instead, we say they suffered from a mental illness that "killed" them. According to the medically and politically correct view, suicide is a public health problem, as if self-killing were a disease that, like diabetes, afflicts X number of persons per 100,000 population.

American antisuicide propaganda makes it appear as if suicide were so frequent as to justify viewing it as an alarming epidemic. Comparison with other countries shows that the opposite is the case: voluntary death is relatively infrequent in America.

According to the World Health Organization's 1997 list "Suicides per 100,000 people per year," the countries with the highest rates are Belarus at 35 per 100,000 and Lithuania and Russia at 30. In midrange are Japan at 24, Hungary at 21, and Switzerland at 18. In the low range are Sweden at 13, Canada at 12, and the United States at 11. Among the lowest are Guatemala and Kuwait at 2 and Syria at 0.1.[4]

From the political-philosophical point of view, it makes no difference whether suicide is rare or frequent. The relative infrequency of suicide in the United States reinforces the view that the American government's massive investment in the suicide prevention business is simply another facet of the government's unquenchable thirst for control and power over the daily lives of the people. The correct name of the document officially titled "The Federal Commitment to Suicide Prevention" ought to be "The Federal Commitment to Deprive Americans of Their Natural Right to Death Control." According to that document:

> In 1999 the U.S. suicide rate was 10.7 completed suicides per 100,000 persons, making it the 11th leading cause of death among all age groups. While *suicide is a public health problem for all segments of the American population,* suicide disproportionately

impacts people of certain ages, ethnic/racial backgrounds, and geographic locations. It is the third leading cause of death among Americans aged 15–24 and the second leading cause of death among those aged 25–34. . . . The suicide rate for older Americans is also troubling at more than 17 suicide deaths per 100,000 persons aged 75 and older.[5]

Note the bureaucratic language, transforming "suicide," an act, into an actor that kills and the self-killer into the victim of a fictitious disease. In this idiom, individuals do not choose to kill themselves; they are killed by suicide. The grandiosity of state-sponsored and state-supported suicide prevention programs complements the grandiosity of state-sponsored and state-supported mental health programs:

Suicide prevention efforts gained important momentum at the national level during the 1990s. During the course of the decade, the grassroots survivor organization Suicide Prevention Advocacy Network (SPAN-USA) formed; the United Nations/ World Health Organization issued the 1996 summary, *Prevention of Suicide: Guidelines for the Formulation and Implementation of National Strategies*; the 105th Congress declared suicide prevention to be a national priority . . . ; the first National Suicide Prevention Conference assembled in Reno, Nevada in 1998; and the Surgeon General issued a *Call to Action to Prevent Suicide*. The Surgeon General's report underscored the importance of *harnessing science to develop safe and effective approaches to suicide prevention* and educating the public about those approaches.[6]

With science added to the mix, no rational person or respectable group can afford to oppose these "medical" programs deemed to be essential for the "health and safety" of the American people. Together with mental health, suicide prevention is a cornucopia of pseudotherapeutic "programs" that deprive people of essential liberties and enrich quacks, posing as "protectors of the health of the people":

> Various HHS [Health and Human Services] operating divisions conduct suicide prevention activities that are consistent with their particular mandates and expertise. . . . The following is a profile of these suicide prevention activities and the inter-agency collaboration among the Substance Abuse and Mental Health Services Administration (SAMHSA); National Institutes of Health (NIH); Centers for Disease Control and Prevention (CDC); Health Resources and Services Administration (HRSA); and Indian Health Service. SAMHSA provides Federal block grants to states in support of mental health and drug abuse services. . . . NIH consists of 27 Institutes and Centers . . . supporting the greatest proportion of suicide-related research.[7]

The public, seemingly uncomprehending, supports these pseudo-medical rituals.

3

"When I am, death is not, and when death is, I am not," declared the Greek philosopher Epicurus (341–270 BCE). Strictly speaking, *death is not a part of our life; only the idea of dying is.* Death is a part of our survivors' lives.

People say they fear death, but, more often than not, they fear dying. Woody Allen's witty remark, "I am not afraid of death, I just don't want to be there when it happens," is just right. The term *mercy death* reflects the widespread understanding that quick and painless death is "better" than prolonged and painful dying. To be sure, there is no objectively "good death" or "bad death"; there is only dying—or living—deemed "good" or bad," according to the values of the person doing the judging.

No one can prevent a person who wants to kill himself from doing so.[8] Everyone knows that. This has not deterred modern societies from entrusting psychiatrists with the duty of preventing suicide and psychiatrists from accepting and embracing this responsibility.

Since it is impossible—except by the most extraordinary means—to prevent a person intent on killing himself from doing so, a market arises in providing such extraordinary means to individuals and institutions whose business is to employ such means. In fact, such a market in the incarceration and incapacitation of "dangerous persons" arose and developed in tandem with the birth and growth of asylum-hospital-inpatient psychiatry. Hence the popular association of straitjackets with madhouses.[9]

Formerly, inquisitors *tortured* people. Today, by quasi definition, no official holder of power tortures. When spy agencies or military forces use torture, we call it *enhanced interrogation* or *fighting the war on terror*. When mental hospitals and psychiatrists use torture, we call it *suicide prevention*.

The registered Internet domain http://www.preventsuicide .com/ advertises a modern straitjacket designed specifically for restraining mental patients deemed to be "dangerous to themselves." Taking for granted the blame-shifting characteristic of our culture, the ad is titled "We Want Your Title to Be 'Officer' not 'Defendant'" and states:

> Inmates on suicide watch in prison need not be completely naked. . . . Safety. Security. Savings. These have been the focus of Ferguson Safety Products since its founding in 1989. Safety: All of the products from Ferguson Safety are specifically designed to keep problem inmates from hurting themselves and creating more headaches for you and your colleagues. . . . Ferguson's Original Safety Smock[s] . . . last years longer and are considerably more tear resistant than cheap knock-offs—saving you

replacement costs, staff time, and lowering your liability by preventing wrongful death lawsuits.

Under ordinary circumstances, people recoil not only from killing themselves but also from the very *idea* of doing so. Many people seem unable or unwilling to accept that some persons sometimes choose to die by their own hands.[10] This is why we often debate whether one or another action or omission should count as suicide or be classified instead as accident, martyrdom, patriotism, self-sacrifice, or the result of mental illness.

In this book I use the word *suicide* in its purely descriptive sense, to refer to the act of deliberately causing one's own death, which I call "autohomicide." If we engage in a sexual act that involves another person, we do not call the act "autoeroticism." Similarly, if we engage in a suicidal act that involves another person, we ought not to call it "autohomicide."

Assisted suicide is heterohomicide, not autohomicide. Like any human action, suicide may be deemed good, bad, or indifferent; praised or condemned; recommended or forbidden; or accepted as we accept the weather.

Of all living beings, only humans have the option of terminating their own lives. Most people now regard this choice as an abhorrent temptation and avoid thinking about it. When they do think about suicide, they view such thinking as something prima facie "abnormal" and readily accept the concept of "suicidal ideation" that, according to Wikipedia, is "a common medical term for thoughts about suicide."[11]

We do not talk about "sex ideation," or "eating ideation," or "divorce ideation." Why do we need the special term *suicidal ideation*? To readily cast it in the category of "psychiatric symptom," which it is the psychiatrist's duty to detect and whose seriousness he is expected to evaluate. Who is fooling whom?

Merriam-Webster's defines *ideation* as a noun: "the capacity for or the act of forming or entertaining ideas <suicidal *ideation*>." This conceptualization is both the cause and the consequence of the psychiatric conception of suicide as psychopathological. Thinking about sex, money, or vacation is "reflection," "longing," "planning," or "pondering," not "ideation." The psychiatric premise that thinking about suicide is a symptom of the disease "clinical depression" is justificatory rhetoric: thinking about suicide is simply thinking, a symptom of freedom of thought. It is also, as Nietzsche famously observed, a tool of self-preservation: "The thought of suicide is a powerful solace. By means of it one gets through many a bad night" (Der Gedanke an den Selbstmord ist ein sehr starkes Trostmittel. Man kommt damit gut über die böse Nacht hinweg). Unfortunately, the English term *solace* lacks many of the significant meanings of the German term *Trostmittel*. *Cassel's* renders *Trost* as "consolation," "comfort," and "solace." *Mittel*, a frequently used term, is "remedy," "medicine," "means," "instrument," and "tool." For example, *Schlafmittel* is "sleeping pill," and *Nahrungsmittel* is "foodstuff." The difference between the psychiatric and Nitzschean concepts of thinking about suicide could not be greater: in psychiatry, it is a disease to be prevented and treated; in Nietzsche, it is a remedy to be appreciated and treasured.

4

As a phenomenon, suicide is ancient. As a medical problem, it is recent. The medicalization of homicide—both auto- and hetero-homicide—is an aspect of the birth and growth of pharmacracy and the therapeutic state.[12]

Medical historians William F. Bynum and Michael Neve observe, "By early Victorian times, suicide had been more or less completely medicalized."[13] What do these writers mean when they use the term *medicalized*? They mean that measles and melanoma are medical problems by nature, whereas masturbation and murder are medical problems by nurture (culture), a distinction competent medical historians take for granted: we do not talk about the medicalization of bodily diseases, such as infections and malignancies, but do talk about the medicalization of mental diseases, such as dangerousness and depression.

Long ago, I suggested that we cannot understand psychiatry unless we are familiar with its history, specifically with the similarities between the religious and medical attitudes toward death, dying, and suicide.[14] In the Judeo-Christian-Islamic worldview, human life is God's gift and property. Suicide is self-murder, *felo de se* (felony against oneself). Inasmuch as the legitimacy of the Christian sovereign's rule rested on his special relationship to God, self-murder was also an offense against him and was accordingly punished by both canon and criminal law.

With suicide defined as a species of murder, the persons sitting in judgment of self-killers had the duty to punish them.

Since punishing suicide required doing injustice to innocent parties—the wives and minor children of the deceased—the task soon proved to be an intolerable burden. In the seventeenth century, men sitting on coroners' juries began to recoil against desecrating the corpse and dispossessing the suicide's dependents of their means of support. However, their religious beliefs precluded repeal of the laws punishing the crime of "self-murder." Their only recourse was to evade the laws: the doctrinal fiction that the self-slayer is, ipso facto, *non compos mentis* and hence not responsible for his act accomplished this task.

The transformation of *self-killing from a deliberate act* into the *unintended consequence of a disease (of the brain)* is an integral part of the pseudoscience of psychiatry and the vastly influential institutions of social control that rest on its claims called "theories" and coercions called "treatments." The "insanitizing of suicide" antecedes the birth of psychiatry. Psychiatry is a result, not the cause, of the transformation of self-murder from sin-crime into illness-excuse.

The impetus for excusing self-murder did not, and could not, come from its beneficiaries, the victims of the law against suicide. The suicide was dead. His family, bereft of means and reputation, was powerless. Instead, the impetus for medicalizing suicide came from those individuals who needed "reforming" the anti-suicide law and possessed the political clout to bring it about: the coroners and the persons on coroners' juries who had the burden of imposing harsh penalties on the corpses of suicides and the widows and orphans they left behind.

Once the medicalization of suicide began, encountering no obstacles, it progressed rapidly. First, the successful suicide's act was redefined as insanity and excused as an *illness*. Then, in the nineteenth and twentieth centuries, the unsuccessful or would-be suicide's act was redefined as a *treatable illness:* he was incarcerated in an insane asylum—later renamed "mental hospital"—ostensibly to prevent his death, actually to punish him for disturbing the orderly functioning of his family and society. Today, so-called suicide prevention is a quasi-medical specialty and a big business. The term *Big Pharma* is part of our everyday language. *Big Psychiatry* and *Big Suicide Prohibition* are labels waiting to be created.

A few words about the legal history of suicide in the West are in order here. After the Christianization of Rome, the Catholic Church adopted the Jewish ban on self-murder as a sin against God, the Creator. In 563, the Council of Braga declared suicide to be self-murder, punished by denial of burial in consecrated ground. Medieval Christian sovereigns added to this the secular penalty of forfeiting the suicide's goods and property. The law of forfeiture remained in force in England until the nineteenth century, albeit, from the eighteenth century on, it was systematically circumvented by excusing the self-killer as, ipso facto, insane. For approximately the past century, rabbinic and church authorities alike have classified suicides as *non compos mentis*, permitting them to receive normal religious burial services.

A century and a half ago, John Stuart Mill famously declared, "Over himself, over his own body and mind, the individual is sovereign."[15] Victorian liberals tried to liberate the *private person* from the despotism of ecclesiastic strictures and social taboos. Little did they realize that their efforts would backfire and that, a century later, old, inherited religious strictures would be replaced by new, invented medical strictures with wider scope and greater vindictiveness.[16]

Death, after all is said, is the most obvious instance of a literal "natural right": it is a "benefit" that, eventually, accrues to all of us. Not by accident, the essence of political liberty—in the classic liberal-libertarian view—is the absence of external coercion limiting our ability to act freely (without depriving others of their freedom). In regard to voluntary death, it is therefore important that we focus on "freedom from" coercive suicide prevention and avoid concepts and phrases such as a "right to die," a "right to death with dignity," or a "right to assisted suicide." Instead, we ought to speak of our right to freedom from suicide prevention.

In previous publications I presented my evidence and reasoning for the belief that *medicalized coercion* is profoundly inimical to the medical ethic of primum non nocere (first do no harm) and is incompatible with the liberal-libertarian idea of a free society.[17] In this book I show that the psychiatric profession's uncompromising commitment to coercion in the name of health—specifically, suicide prevention—is tantamount to its self-identification as an enemy of human dignity, personal responsibility, and individual liberty.

1

Suicide Prohibition

1

Diseases are *prevented*. Crimes are *prohibited*. Our systematic mislabeling of suicide prohibition as suicide prevention is incontrovertible evidence of linguistic distortion in the service of medical-statist ideology. The essay "Youth Suicide" on the Web site of the US Centers for Disease Control and Prevention begins with this declarative statement: "Suicide (i.e., taking one's own life) is a serious public health problem that affects even young people." Neither that statement nor Camus' famous declaration that "there is but one truly serious philosophical problem, and that is suicide" is literally true, and every educated person knows it.[1] Both are recommendations concerning how the speaker wants us to view the phenomenon before us.

Why is it important to call coercive-punitive interference with taking one's own life *"suicide prohibition"*? Because suicide is action-doing, not disease-enduring; because the basic tool of the state is coercion, not care; and because the principal method of suicide prevention is incarceration, not information.

Preventive measures are aimed at keeping undesirable *events*, such as accidents and diseases, from happening. Prohibitions are aimed at preventing *persons* from engaging in behaviors defined as "dangerous," such as deliberate harm to others ("crime") or to self ("mental illness"). The difference between these two modes of

13

influencing others is illustrated by the difference between the "war on drugs" and the "war on cancer." The former is fought with guns and prisons, the latter with medical technology and advertising.

Suicide is no longer illegal. But it is forbidden. We have decriminalized it and transferred its control to psychiatry. We deal with suicide and "suicidality" as mental health problems and "treat" them with deprivation of liberty called "hospitalization." However, suicidality is an inclination, not a fact, much less a medical condition. Neither the *act* of killing onself nor the *inclination* to commit the deed is a disease.

Driving while intoxicated (DWI) and killing oneself are both acts or deeds. The inclination-intention to engage in drunk driving is neither a crime nor a mental illness. We have neither criminal nor mental health laws aimed at its *prevention*. Laws against DWI *punish* the deed, not the inclination.

In the seventeenth and eighteenth centuries, this was also the case with respect to suicide: the act was punished; the inclination was ignored.[2] We have inverted that situation, penalizing the inclination, but not the deed, though we still stigmatize it. In a more liberal-libertarian society, neither would be the business of the law, the doctor, or the politician. Today, once a person enters into a professional relationship with a psychiatrist, he becomes, ipso facto, a "mental patient" and ceases to be a person possessing normal rights and responsibilities. Such a person forfeits his right of self-ownership, and the psychiatrist acquires the duty to protect him from himself and others from him. Should the psychiatrist deem the patient to be a danger to himself or others, the psychiatrist is professionally obligated to initiate violence against him, called "suicide prevention" and "civil commitment."

As a result, the psychiatrist also becomes subject to the desires of the patient's relatives. Although professional jargon and social convention conceal it, one of the psychiatrist's functions is to help family members with more power to control their relatives with less power, traditionally by confinement in an asylum, sanatorium, madhouse, or mental hospital and, today, also by coercively drugging them with domesticating chemicals.[3]

Many people recognize that our everyday language refracts social reality in accordance with the prevailing zeitgeist. However, as long as a person remains unentangled in the state's psychiatric control system and is not directly exposed to its actual functioning, he is unlikely to appreciate its threat to basic human rights. Once he becomes a "mental health consumer," he is considered credible only if he praises the system. If he criticizes it, he is dismissed as lacking insight into his illness.

The psychiatric perspective on life began to seep into the zeitgeist of modern Western culture toward the end of the eighteenth century and was ripe when Freud arrived on the scene, in the 1880s. His influence lay mainly in his successful elaboration and popularization of the language of psychopathology and psychotherapy. By the time Freud died, in 1939, W. H. Auden was moved to offer this perceptive tribute to him:

> if often he was wrong and, at times, absurd,
> to us he is no more a person
> now but a whole climate of opinion
> under whom we conduct our different lives.[4]

How and why did our psychiatric-regulatory system come into being? It arose, in the West, as part of, and in tandem with, the Enlightenment and the decline of religion and regulations based on status relations. In modern free societies, the law is expected to treat persons—including doctors and patients—as contracting individuals, not as members of status groups (male or female, rich or poor, well or sick, black or white).

In November 2010, a feature article in the journal *Physicians Practice* was titled "Is It Ever OK to Lie to Patients?" The author, journalist Shelly K. Schwartz, emphasized the relatively recent change in the doctor-patient relationship from paternalism and lies to contract and truth sharing:

> Informed consent wasn't always the mantra. Thirty years ago, cancer patients in the United States were frequently misled about the extent of their illness. "I remember being in medical school years ago and being distinctly told that when a person has lung cancer, never tell them they have lung cancer," says Peter Dixon, a former oncologist and current primary-care doctor. . . . "We were told to give them a dose of morphine and wash our hands of it. Things have certainly changed." Today, doctors are expected to treat patients as partners, delivering a complete picture of their prognosis and treatment options so patients can take an active role in their own healthcare. . . . If there's one thing sacred in the doctor-patient relationship, it's trust. Open and honest dialogue on both sides of the exam table is by all accounts critical to effective care. . . . Indeed, patient autonomy is the cornerstone of modern medicine and patient-centered care. Aside from the ethical mandate of truth telling in the modern age of medicine, physicians in most states are also legally obligated to disclose all relevant health information to patients.[5]

2

Psychiatry and psychoanalysis arose in the era of medical paternalism, and their practitioners have held on to its deceptions in a veritable death grip. Psychiatrists and psychoanalysts agree, and always agreed, in their opposition to relating to "patients" as competent adults, and for similar reasons, albeit differently formulated: psychiatrists, because they view the mentally ill as more or less incompetent; psychoanalysts, because they view everyone, except themselves, as puppets of their unconscious impulses.

These concepts and images are the sine qua nons for justifying psychiatric oppression and psychoanalytic domination. Since the 1960s, this political ugliness—intrinsic to the mental health professions—has come under attack.[6] As a result, mental health professionals have escalated their claim that it is their moral obligation to paternalistically "protect" their patients. In 2003, Marcia Goin, a psychoanalyst and then president of the American Psychiatric Association (APA), declared, "We can make contracts with builders, insurers, and car dealers, but not with patients."[7]

Why can't psychiatrist contract with their patients? Because contracting implies two (or more) legally equal parties, each putting his cards on the table. It implies mutual obligations, each party having legal power to compel his partner to fulfill the contract or compensate him for failure to do so.

What moved Goin to offer such an unqualified rejection of psychiatrists' contractual relations with their patients? She offered her comment in connection with the so-called no-suicide contract, a product of the policy of coercive psychiatric suicide prevention. The term refers to the psychiatrist's promise that he will not commit the patient in return for the patient's promise to not kill himself. Why should the psychiatrist ask the patient to promise him such a thing? The "no-suicide contract" is a priori nonsensical. Oncologists are no strangers to voluntary death. Not expected to lock up their potentially suicidal patients, they are not concerned with suicide contracts. The only obligation a "normal" patient has to a "normal" doctor is to pay his bill. He need not ingest the drugs the doctor prescribes or follow his recommendations. Why should the psychiatrist's relationship with his patient deviate from this pattern and descend to the pattern characteristic of the relationship between parents and young children? A recent textbook, *Emergency Psychiatry,* published by the American Psychiatric Association, explains:

The suicide prevention contract, also known as the no-harm contract, was originally developed in 1973 to facilitate the management of the patient at suicide risk. Even today, clinicians readily report that patients are either able or unable to "consent for their safety." However, despite the widespread use of verbal and written suicide contracts in clinical practice, no studies have proved their effectiveness in reducing or preventing suicide. Clinicians should be warned that such suicide prevention contracts are based on subjective rather than objective evidence, are not legally binding, and should not serve as a substitute for careful clinical assessment.[8]

Contracting governs relations between nonpsychiatric physicians and their patients. It does not govern relations between psychiatric physicians and their patients. Psychiatrists proudly reject the ethics of commerce in favor of what they regard as the loftier ethics of care. The seller of plumbing services is obligated to deliver only that which his customer requests and he promises to provide. The seller of psychiatric services is obligated to deliver more: he must protect the customer from himself and others from the customer.

To understand psychiatrists' preference for paternalistic status relations over egalitarian contract relations, it is helpful to be familiar with the work of Sir Henry James Sumner Maine (1822–88), the great English historian and legal scholar. In *Ancient Law*, the book for which he is famous, Maine offered this important observation:

> The movement of the progressive societies has been uniform in one respect. Through all its course it has been distinguished by the gradual dissolution of family dependency and the growth of *individual obligation* in its place. . . . Nor is it difficult to see what the tie between man and man which replaces by degrees those forms of reciprocity in rights and duties which have their origin in the Family. *It is Contract.* Starting, as from one terminus of history, from a condition of society in which all the

relations of Persons are summed up in the relations of Family, we seem to have steadily moved towards a phase of social order in which all these relations arise from the free agreement of individuals. In Western Europe the progress achieved in this direction has been considerable. Thus the *status of the Slave has disappeared—it has been superseded by the contractual relation of the servant to his master.* The status of the Female under Tutelage, if the tutelage be understood of persons other than her husband, has also ceased to exist; from her coming of age to her marriage all the relations she may form are relations of contract. . . . The apparent exceptions are exceptions of that stamp which illustrate the rule. The child before years of discretion, the orphan under guardianship, *the adjudged lunatic,* have all their capacities and incapacities regulated by the Law of Persons. But why? The reason is differently expressed in the conventional language of different systems, but in substance it is stated to the same effect by all. The great majority of Jurists are constant to the principle that the classes of persons just mentioned are subject to extrinsic control on the single ground that they do not possess the faculty of forming a judgment on their own interests; in other words, that they are wanting in the first essential of an engagement by Contract. The word Status may be usefully employed to construct a formula expressing the law of progress thus indicated. . . . *[W]e may say that the movement of the progressive societies has hitherto been a movement from Status to Contract.*[9]

The movement from status to contract is a theme dramatically displayed in the American War of Independence and the birth and growth of the United States of America.

3

If there is a single word that captures the idea of the United States of America, that word is *freedom.* In colonial times, the term meant primarily *freedom from control by distant, powerful individuals and institutions,* particularly the Roman pope and Vatican and the British king and Parliament, both symbols of dreaded despotism.

The theme of our national anthem, "The Star-Spangled Banner," is emblematic of our glorification of freedom, rather than such competing political values as justice or equality. The anthem's lyrics, composed by Francis Scott Key in 1814, are based on a poem, "Defense of Fort McHenry." Key had witnessed the bombardment of the fort by Royal Navy ships in Chesapeake Bay during the battle of Baltimore in the War of 1812. Each of the anthem's stanzas ends with the refrain "land of the free and the home of the brave."[10]

In the early days of the Republic, nothing could have been further from the minds of Americans than the idea that it is the obligation of the federal government to protect them from themselves. "The provisions we have made [for our government]," wrote Jefferson to Lord North in 1775, "are such as please ourselves; they answer the substantial purposes of government and of justice, and other purposes than these should not be answered." People who want to be free to govern themselves do not erect a legal framework empowering their government to incarcerate them should they—in the opinion of government-paid medical bureaucrats—become "mentally ill and dangerous to themselves or others."

What was so important about freedom as self-government for eighteenth-century Americans? That it made possible the flourishing of the individual and the family. People then had a keen recognition that when despotism rules, there can be no self-government: self-government can exist only when government is limited. The idea of "limited government" is thus an essential element of the idea of America as the land of the free. In its original intent, the term *limited government* meant *independence* from authoritarian-despotic interference in the conduct of everyday life.

Exactly what is despotism? It is the political condition characterized by a single individual—the *despot*—wielding all the authority, legitimacy, and power in the community or state. This form of despotism was common in the first forms of statehood—for example, in ancient Egypt. In Byzanthium, "despot"—from the ancient Greek *despotes* (literally, *the master*)—was an imperial title. For us today, the word *despotism* has a pejorative meaning. However, that was not its meaning for people who believed it was the God-given, "natural" way of the world.

For Americans, the importance of the ideas of limited and unlimited governments cannot be overemphasized. The Declaration of Independence indicts the British government of the sin of despotism: "But when a long train of abuses and usurpations, pursuing invariably the same Object, evinces a design to reduce them under absolute Despotism, it is their [the people's] right, it is their duty, to throw off such Government. . . . A Prince, whose character is thus marked by every act which may define a Tyrant, is unfit to be the ruler of a free people."

> The Founders justified their decision to *secede*—that is, *separate*—from "the mother country" with these immortal words:
>
> We hold these truths to be self-evident, that all men are created equal, that they are endowed by their Creator with certain unalienable Rights, that among these are Life, Liberty and the pursuit of Happiness. That to secure these rights, Governments are instituted among Men, deriving their just powers from the consent of the governed,—That whenever any Form of Government becomes destructive of these ends, it is the Right of the People to alter or to abolish it, and to institute new Government, laying its foundation on such principles and organizing its powers in such form, as to them shall seem most likely to effect their Safety and Happiness.

A near synonym for *limited government* is *enumerated powers*. Article 1, Section 8, of the Constitution *enumerates* the powers of Congress:

> The Congress shall have power To lay and collect taxes, duties, imposts and excises, to pay the debts and provide for the common defence and general welfare of the United States; but all duties, imposts and excises shall be uniform throughout the United States; To borrow money on the credit of the United States; To regulate commerce with foreign nations, and among the several states, and with the Indian tribes; To establish a uniform rule of naturalization, and uniform laws on the subject of bankruptcies throughout the United States; To coin money, regulate the value thereof, and of foreign coin, and fix the standard of weights and measures; etc.[11]

In short, the term *enumerated powers* refers to a list of government functions granted to the United States Congress by the Constitution and *limiting the scope of federal government* to those functions.

4

Although regulating suicide is clearly not among Congress's "enumerated powers," dying voluntarily is now regarded as one of the government's major public health problems, and its prevention is a gargantuan government-funded industry. A policy statement, titled "Federal Commitment to Suicide Prevention," issued in 2003 by the US government, begins with this introduction: "Each year approximately 30,000 lives are lost to suicide in the United States. Yet, this disturbing loss of American lives is preventable. The US Department of Health and Human Services (HHS) is working to prevent suicide and its devastating impact on families, friends, and communities. HHS funds an array of initiatives that examine incidence, research risk and protective factors, evaluate prevention programs, and promote effective program models."[12]

Not every death is a "disturbing loss," nor is every suicide "preventable." No one determined to kill himself can be prevented from doing so. Individuals incarcerated in prisons and mental hospitals on "suicide watch" frequently kill themselves. Even prisoners on death row manage to do so: we call that "cheating the hangman," demonstrating that the true purpose of the death penalty is dramatizing the principle that only the state possesses the legitimate authority to deliberately kill a person. If the goal of the death penalty was simply to terminate the condemned person's life, it could be achieved more ethically and easily by providing the prisoner with a lethal dose of the appropriate drug and letting him kill himself.[13] The legal system needs neither professional nor medical executioners. Nevertheless, psychiatrists clamor for the power to prevent suicide and provide "suicide assistance."

Like psychiatrists, educational authorities deny the true consequences of suicide prevention—in their case for college students—and persist in restating their medicalized mendacities. In the spring of 2010, Cornell University president David J. Skorton, spooked by three suicides within a period of a few months, "took out a full-page ad in the campus paper, *The Cornell Daily Sun*, saying: 'Your well-being is the foundation on which your success is built. If you learn anything at Cornell, please learn to ask for help.'"[14] The stupid know how to ask for help without going to college. The smart need to go to Cornell to learn to do so.

Skorton's language illustrates the insincere, bureaucratic-therapeutic rhetoric of the suicide prohibitionists: "On and off campus, there is an epidemic of suicide among young people. As a father, teacher, physician and president of a university where we have recently experienced the horror of multiple suicides, I have long been concerned about this national public health crisis."

Every death is a crisis for the affected family, but three deaths, or thirty deaths, do not constitute an "epidemic" or a "national public health crisis" in a nation of three hundred million people. "What is the way ahead? . . . [W]e need more research into the factors that lead to suicide in this age group and how to identify those at greatest risk. . . . [S]tudents must learn that it is smart to ask for help."[15] Suicide by college student is not the sort of problem that could be "solved" by "research." The advice that the college student frightened to death by the life task ahead of him should seek help from mental health professionals working for the college is ill-advised or ill-intentioned. The primary loyalty of the college's mental health professional is to the institution that pays his salary, not the student whose behavior threatens its reputation and financial well-being. (The parents of students who kill themselves regularly sue the college and usually collect millions in damages.)[16] From the viewpoint of the school, the best "therapy" for the suicidal student is to get him off the campus and liberate the college from the burden of having to protect the student from himself.

Each time several students on the same campus kill themselves within a few months, it is an "epidemic" and a major embarrassment for the school. On November 13, 2010, a feature story in the *Washington Post* was titled "Third Suicide This Year at William & Mary Highlights Challenges of Prevention."[17] What the story highlights is not the "challenges of suicide prevention," but that there *is no such thing as suicide prevention*. Yet, after each such episode, the same ritual, using the same liturgy, is repeated:

> It was the third apparent suicide this calendar year at the College of William and Mary, leaving the school grappling with questions about what could have prompted the deaths and how another one might be prevented. . . . [T]here is no way of knowing how the three deaths at William and Mary compare with other schools because no independent group compares suicide rates at colleges and universities. Still, William and Mary, an elite state university with nearly 8,000 students in Virginia's Tidewater region, responded with major new initiatives on campus. College officials dispatched grief counselors. And the student government put notes on dorm-room doors warning of the signs of severe depression. "Even if these aren't people we know directly, you always know someone who knew them,"

said Wesley Ng, president of a student health group. "It's scary when it touches you so closely. . . . A lot of people are asking why, what could I have done?" . . . The student newspaper, the *Flat Hat*, raised questions about a decades-old label with this headline: "Surge in deaths leaves College battling reputation as a 'suicide school.'" College officials say such suggestions are unfair. . . . Campus suicide awareness campaigns often have focused on getting students comfortable with using words such as "depression" and dispelling myths about the counseling center. . . . When a student is having a mental health crisis, health professionals and administrators assess the student and make a plan of action. That sometimes includes a leave from school. "They could be doing straight-A work, but we have to focus on their medical issues first," said Virginia Ambler, William and Mary's vice president of student affairs. "The goal always is to get a student to a point where they can succeed." [William and Mary's dean of students] Patricia Volp added: "And be alive."

I wonder what "myths" the writer refers to and why there are myths about the counseling center but evidently no myths about the medical dispensary or swim team. I surmise the "myth" is that the counseling center paves the way out of a coveted college rather than into "mental health." "'None of the students on this campus want to have problems,' said Caitlin Goldblatt, a senior literary and cultural studies major. . . . 'They want to be perfect.'"

One must pity such students. They have a very long way to go in their growing up. Having to grow up in a nation in which "the number of college students who have mental illnesses increases each year, as improved diagnoses and medication make it easier for them to stay in school and manage campus life," makes their task only harder.

What accounts for the systematic mendacity of social authorities about suicide and suicide prevention? The need to conceal that their aim is *control, not care, and punishment, not protection.*

5

The following narratives are based on the court records of individuals unappreciative of the lifesaving suicide prevention services they received.

In 2006, RF filed a petition in a Pennsylvania court "to expunge his civil commitment record."[18] After his petition was denied, he appealed, and his appeal was denied: "The Superior Court . . . held that sufficient evidence supported former committee's initial involuntary civil commitment, as well as his extended commitment, such that he was not entitled to expungement of his civil commitment record." How did RF get into his predicament?

> Appellant became the focus of inquiry when he phoned a suicide hotline ("New Hope Health Clinic") on the 17th of April, 2004, and asked if the service sold information on various ways to commit suicide. . . . In advance of calling the hotline, Appellant went to the "Google" web site and keyed in the search phrase "suicide, how to commit." Appellant then clicked on the first link at the top of the "Google" page. . . . On the second page of the web site, Appellant downloaded the following, as herein relevant: How To Commit Suicide.

After speaking to the suicide hotline operator for a few minutes, RF hung up, and the operator notified the state police, as required by law: "The clear and central intent of the general assembly in enacting the Mental Health Procedures Act was to assure that those individuals who are severely mentally disabled will be provided with the medical care they need, for their own health and safety, and for the safety of others."

> Pennsylvania State Trooper Howard J. Bloomfield was dispatched to Appellant's home. . . . After the passage of a few minutes, the trooper observed Appellant looking out the garage

window. A few minutes later, Appellant opened the garage
door and walked toward the trooper, who advised Appellant
that the state police had been alerted that someone had placed
a phone call threatening to commit suicide, being in possession
of a loaded rifle, not to send the police, and the call was traced
to Appellant's home. Despite repeated pleadings by the trooper
that Appellant was not under arrest, not in any trouble, and the
police were just seeking the truth, Appellant denied making
any phone call.

Now Trooper Bloomfield was in charge. He had to determine
whether to detain RF on suspicion of being dangerous to himself
or others and transport him to the nearest insane asylum or drop
the matter, return to his barracks, and be blamed and punished
if RF killed himself. RF had entered—or, more precisely, was successfully entrapped in—what Chekhov called the "enchanted
circle" from which there is no escape: "The circumstances surrounding the suicide hotline call . . . convinced Trooper Bloomfield to transport Appellant to the Pocono Medical Center for
evaluation. En route to the hospital, Appellant admitted that
he was depressed and going through a divorce. . . . Once at the
Pocono Medical Center, Trooper Bloomfield completed an 'Application For Involuntary Emergency Examination And Treatment'
pursuant to Section 7302 of the Mental Health Procedures Act."

Thereafter, RF was processed according to the rules of the
mental health bureaucracy. Henceforth, no one in the system
could afford to be interested in him as a human being in distress.
Everyone followed the bureaucratically prescribed rules for dealing with such a "dangerous mental patient," protecting himself
from the "patient's" unpredictable, "mentally ill" action:

> The involuntary commitment papers filed by Trooper Bloom-
> field resulted in an examination by Doctor DeFranco . . . [who]
> found that Appellant exhibited "suicidal ideation." . . . Further,

the doctor opined: "The patient is severely mentally disabled and in need of treatment. He should be admitted to a facility . . . for a period of treatment not to exceed 120 hours." . . . [When that period expired] a Section 7303 hearing was conducted by a mental health review officer to determine whether Appellant's stay in the psychiatric unit should be extended beyond the initial involuntary commitment of 120 hours. Doctor Abdo Saba, a psychiatrist, examined Appellant after his admission, which session resulted in the patient admitting feeling depressed, having suicidal thoughts, and calling a phone number on the internet to secure "more details about ways [on] how to commit suicide." These suicidal ideations appeared to be rooted in the fact that Appellant was "going through a lot of stress, mostly [because] he was going through [a] divorce, and he was given 60 days to leave the house." . . . The doctor also reported that the patient refused to take a prescribed antidepressant. . . . *Dr. Saba was afraid* "the patient would get more depressed and carry out his suicidal thought." (Emphasis added)

After a few weeks' confinement, RF was released. A year later he filed a petition to have his commitment expunged. The court record continues:

As discussed above, a person can be involuntarily committed when he is "severely mentally disabled." Further, persons are classified as severely mentally disabled when their ability to exercise self-control or to care for themselves is so lessened that they pose "a clear and present danger of harm to others" or themselves. . . . Clear and present danger to himself shall be shown by establishing that within the past 30 days . . . the person has attempted suicide and that there is the reasonable probability of suicide unless adequate treatment is afforded under this act. . . . Appellant had phoned a suicide hotline to quench his "curiosity" on the methodology of committing suicide, which phone number was secured from a web site accessed using the

key words: "suicide, how to commit." Appellant also conceded
to the hotline operator that he had contemplated suicide, was in
possession of a loaded weapon, wanted to do it "right," and not
to send the police because they would be denied entry into his
home. Couple these events with the fact that Appellant admitted being depressed because of his impending divorce and
removal from the house within 60 days. . . . We find that the
trooper was in possession of sufficient facts (articulated in the
involuntary commitment papers at Pocono Medical Center) constituting "reasonable grounds" to believe that Appellant was
severely mentally disabled and in need of immediate treatment
because he presented a "clear and present danger" to himself.
To explicate, Appellant used the internet to access ways to commit suicide, and he phoned a suicide hotline to gather further
information on the subject, which we find coalesce to constitute
proof in furtherance of Appellant's suicidal ideation. . . . Sub
judice, we find that Appellant's suicidal ideations were noted by
Dr. DeFranco in the Section 7302 documents, as well as by Dr.
Saba in the Section 7303 documents and during his testimony
at the Section 7303 hearing. . . . Dr. Saba [stated]: "Patient came
in on 302 petitioned by the police that patient had suicidal ideas
and he had multiple loaded weapon[s] at home. Patient has been
isolated on the unit refusing his medication, sad expression,
pacing, hesitant, not being truthful about the place and number
of guns he has at home. . . . *I'm afraid* that under these circumstances that [Appellant] would get more depressed and carry
out his suicidal thoughts. . . . *I have great concern* that [Appel-
lant is in] danger to hurt himself or hurt somebody else, and
I'm asking the [mental health review officer] for 30 days or more
for observation, for stabilization, before [Appellant] leaves the
hospital." (Emphasis added)

The record speaks for itself. I want to note only that RF's
"hospitalization" was a charade: he was free to kill himself in
the hospital and after he was discharged. He was not free to kill

himself without first being duly processed into a "certified mental patient." The psychiatrists feared not that RF would kill himself but that he would do so under circumstances that would expose them to bureaucratic censure or legal penalties. The court concluded, "Accordingly, in light of the preceding, we find no merit to any of Appellant's claims seeking to expunge evidence of his involuntary commitment under Section 7302 and Section 7303 of the Mental Health Procedures Act."

6

A psychiatric finding of "dangerousness to self" is the *attribution* of future "dangerousness" to an innocent person. It is an incrimination masquerading as a diagnosis. No one can prove to his adversaries that, in the future, he will not be dangerous or be deemed dangerous by others. The "diagnosis" of "dangerousness to self or others" is the ideal tactic for justifying involuntary mental hospitalization: it forms the backbone of the commitment process. One more example of the Kafkaesque judicial-psychiatric procedure that undergirds such incarceration must suffice. The gist of the case summarized below was summed up by the court in the following astonishingly candid words: "Todd, J. [Judge], held that: extended involuntary commitment does not require a demonstration of an overt act within the past 30 days."[19]

On August 26, 1999, "SB was admitted involuntarily to The Meadows Psychiatric Center." Subsequently, SB converted her involuntary admission to a voluntary admission. A month later, when she wanted to leave, "the Meadows filed an application for extended involuntary treatment. . . . A hearing was held on September 23, 1999 before a Mental Health Review Officer (MHRO), who determined that SB was in need of continued treatment and recommended that SB be involuntarily committed for a period of no more than twenty days."

On September 23, 1999, SB filed a Petition for Review of the Certification. The trial court denied the petition, and she appealed. According to the court record:

> SB presents the following issue for this Court's review: Whether due process protections require a Mental Health Review Officer to make a finding of an overt act within the past thirty days in a Mental Health Procedures Act §303 hearing? . . . In the present case, we are called upon only to interpret the statute. . . . Turning now to SB's contention that involuntary commitment under Section 303 requires a demonstration of an overt act within the past thirty days, we note that . . . if the judge or the review officer finds that the person is severely mentally disabled and in need of continued involuntary treatment, he shall so certify. . . . A person is severely mentally disabled when, as a result of mental illness . . . *he poses a clear and present danger of harm to others or to himself.* . . . SB argued that an "involuntary commitment under Section 303 requires a finding of an overt act within the past thirty days."

The court rejected SB's argument, noting that a psychiatric nurse at the Meadows testified that SB

> refused to take her medication for depression and anxiety, and . . . was unable to "contract for safety," a procedure by which a patient agrees to approach the staff for help if she feels suicidal. . . . We also find that the language of this Court in In re S.C. suggests, despite S.B.'s argument to the contrary, that no overt act is necessary. . . . Thus, the language of this Court in In re S.C. clearly suggests that an individual may be involuntarily committed . . . absent a showing of an overt act. . . . In re R.D., . . . [the court] found that evidence that the appellant was refusing to eat and refusing to take her psychotropic medication was sufficient proof under the clear and convincing standard that [appellant] was "severely mentally disabled." . . . This holding is the only logical result in that where an individual

previously has been committed and under the supervision of mental health care providers, such as in the instant case, the goal of the providers is to prevent additional overt acts which present a clear and present danger to the individual.

I surmise that many people who read these case histories cringe with embarrassment at the humiliation of the subjects, who have harmed no one yet were compelled to endure the psychiatrists' "care." Decent doctors do not humiliate their patients. Decent psychiatrists owe their patients no less.[20]

7

It was not always thus and need not remain thus. If enough psychiatrists had the decency to refuse humiliating their patients, they could, at a minimum, split psychiatry into two parts, one serving the patient's self-defined interests, the other serving the family's, employer's, and legal system's interests.[21]

The prohibition of voluntary death began in the eighteenth century, when the successful suicide's act was attributed to and excused as an *illness*, called *insanity*. In the nineteenth and twentieth centuries, this idea was extended to encompass the would-be or unsuccessful suicide. Defined as a *patient suffering from a preventable and treatable illness*, the person *suspected of suicidal ideation* was incarcerated in an insane asylum or mental hospital, ostensibly to prevent his death, actually to punish him for disturbing the orderly functioning of his family and society.

Paradoxically, it was safer to be suicidal in the eighteenth century than it is in the twenty-first. By way of contrast, then, let us take a brief look at the "suicidality" of the famous writer and early feminist activist Mary Wollstonecraft (1759–97).

Born in London to a middle-class family, Wollstonecraft learned to read and write at home, received some education in a girls day school, but, for the most part, was self-educated, indeed "self-made." The result was a hardworking, brilliant, accomplished, and unhappy person. Author of *A Vindication of the Rights of Woman* (1792) and other works, Wollstonecraft is an important figure in eighteenth-century intellectual and political history.

In 1793, while in Paris, Wollstonecraft met and fell in love with Gilbert Imlay (1754–1821), a successful American adventurer-businessman. A year later, she bore a daughter whom she named Frances (Fanny) Imlay (1794–1816), although she and Imlay were never married. In May 1795, Wollstonecraft took an overdose of laudanum, was saved, and resumed her tumultuous life.

In October of the same year, she made a more serious suicide attempt by throwing herself into the Thames, an act that could have been fatal.

After Wollstonecraft recovered from her laudanum overdose, she was not assumed to be "depressed" and received no medical "help": no one tried to prevent her from trying to kill herself again. She returned to her literary and social life, married journalist-philosopher William Godwin (1756–1836), had another daughter, and died of puerperal fever. The child was Mary Wollstonecraft Godwin (1797–1851), later Mary Shelley, author of *Frankenstein* and many other works. A neighbor of Wollstonecraft's left the following record of her second suicide attempt: "She took a boat and was rowed to Putney, where going on shore and to the Bridge, she threw herself into the water. Her clothes buoyed her up and she floated, and was taken senseless abt. 200 yards from the Bridge, and by proper applications restored to life. Her mind is now calm; she is separated from Imlay, and visits her friends as usual, and does not object to mention of her attempt."[22]

Janet Todd, one of Wollstonecraft's biographers, cites this description in her notes. In the text, she quotes from a contemporary account in the *Times,* which discreetly elides the "Lady's" name: "Being carried to an inn at Fulham, [she] was soon restored by the skill of one of the medical persons belonging to the Humane Society. . . . In about two hours afterwards, her coach came, with her maid, and a proper change of apparel, when she was conveyed home, perfectly recovered."[23]

Revealingly, Todd seizes on the presence of a "medical man" at the scene and uses that circumstance to rewrite the history of the Royal Humane Society (RHS) and the history of the suicide prevention movement. She presents this account of the suicide attempt: "Unconscious, she [Wollstonecraft] floated downstream, until pulled out of the river by fishermen, doubtless used to suicides. . . . The Royal Humane Society had been set up to pursue the enlightened policy of thwarting self-murders by receiving and, if possible, resuscitating bodies floating down the Thames."[24]

This is a blatant falsification of history. The RHS had nothing to do with "thwarting self-murders." Its founders celebrated bystanders' bravery for saving, often at their own peril, accidentally endangered lives. The self-identification of the society was plain and precise: "Recognising the Bravery of People." This was not the aim of the American Foundation for Suicide Prevention (AFSP). Its founders medicalized suicide and justified its coercive prevention. The modern term *suicide prevention*—a euphemism for the use of the legally authorized force necessary for hindering people from ending their lives voluntarily—suggests cowardice rather than bravery by bystanders. The RHS's Web site states:

> The Royal Humane Society is a charity that grants awards for acts of bravery in the saving of human life and, also, for the restoration of life by resuscitation. Awards may be granted to those who have put their own lives at risk to save or attempt to save someone else. . . . The Society may also give recognition to those who have contributed to the saving or attempted saving of life, though they may not have put their own life at risk. In these instances, a Certificate of Commendation may

be granted. . . . Incidents that have taken place anywhere in the world are considered and anyone of any nationality can be nominated. . . . The Society was founded in London in 1774 by two eminent medical men, William Hawes and Thomas Cogan, who were keen to promote techniques of resuscitation. It became apparent that people were putting their own lives in danger rescuing others and awards were given in recognition of these acts of bravery. This remains the purpose of the society today.[25]

Reference to suicide prevention is conspicuously absent in this statement. The aims of the RHS were, and remain, similar to the aims of modern lifesaving methods such as cardiopulmonary resuscitation or abdominal thrusting (the so-called Heimlich maneuver). Conceptually, these interventions belong to the practice and study of respiratory therapy, pulmonary medicine, and emergency medicine, not to the practice and study of psychiatry, suicidology, or suicide prevention. Commingling the philosophy of the RHS with the philosophy of modern suicide prevention organizations, such as the AFSP, corrupts the commonsense distinction between "saving" as helping and liberating and saving as harming and controlling, and it conflates enabling persons to live life with disabling persons from ending it. The AFSP Web site states:

In 1987, a number of leading experts on suicide came together with business and community leaders and survivors of suicide to form AFSP, a registered 501(c)(3) nonprofit organization. They believed that only a combined effort would make it possible to fund the research necessary for progress in the prevention of suicide. Such an approach has proven successful with heart disease, cancer and diabetes and it was hoped that it would be successful in dealing with depression and suicide. . . . Suicide is now the second major cause of death among high school and

college students. Suicide is even more frequent among older
people. The highest rates are found in men over 50. Before the
AFSP was formed, there was no national not-for-profit organization dedicated to funding the research, education and treatment programs necessary to prevent suicide. Over the past 20
years, we have changed that.[26]

The logical weakness and moral ugliness of this analogy are
obvious. The fact that suicide may cause death is hardly enough to
render the act a "disease like any other." The treatment of medical
patients requires their consent, whereas the prevention of suicide
entails their coercion. The RHS rewards bravery by lay bystanders whose intervention saves lives endangered accidentally. The
AFSP rewards the cowardliness of mental health professionals
who deprive persons whom they deem suicidal of liberty and
define themselves as heroic fighters for health.

8

The contemporary taboo against voluntary death rests heavily
on the idea of mental illness.[27] No piece of misinformation in
America today is more firmly entrenched than the idea that suicide is the manifestation or "symptom" of "clinical depression," a
preventable and treatable "medical disease." This premise leads
to the legitimation of a wide range of psychiatric coercions as
"suicide prevention" measures. We have abolished old racial and
sexual taboos and have replaced them with a new taboo, against
suicide. This is why we are afraid to face it coolly, name it cor-
rectly, talk about it clearly and plainly, and free ourselves of the
moral and legal tentacles in which we have entangled ourselves.
Sadly, instead of serving at least in part as a counterweight
against a popular misconception, the press champions the taboo-
ification of suicide.

The stock in trade of the contemporary psychiatric propagandist is the enthusiastic endorsement of the psychiatric claim that suicide is a symptom of depression by dramatizing stories about "unnecessary suicides" and "wasted lives." "A Life on the Decline, and Then the 'Why?'" is the title of a 2009 essay by the successful writer and mental health mouthpiece Michael Winerip.[28]

In the late 1970s, Steven Schnipper—a gay graphic designer— left his home in Summit, New Jersey, for Manhattan. "He loved museums, architecture, reading, first edition books, the theater, seeing four movies in one day . . . the clothes at Barneys, Bergdorf and Armani; cosmetics counters, face creams, spas, manicures and pedicures; travel; five-star hotels . . . Helvetica typeface; the simple beauty of a straight, clean line. His brother Scott, five years younger, would visit and wonder how the Schnippers had produced such an aesthete."

Initially, Schnipper, whose "art and expression and culture and sophistication and taste stood out," was successful: he held well-paying jobs at Estée Lauder, creating "packaging, brochures, advertising, in-store displays and direct mailings that looked like fine art." His first lover and lifelong best friend, Wesley Mancini, a fabric designer, said, "His 40s were definitely the best decade of his life."

Schnipper lived in a one-bedroom condo in the heart of Chelsea's gay community. "He supported the Gay Men's Health Crisis, marched yearly in the AIDS walks and volunteered to deliver food to a senior center in the West Village." Winerip describes Schnipper's Manhattan-style gay life as near perfect. Then, in his fifties, his world began to fall apart:

In 2003, during a round of downsizing, he was let go after 20 years at Estée Lauder. He quickly found work as a creative director at Revlon, but after three years lost his job there, too. . . . He was hired by Coty, but let go in 2007, and never worked steadily again. He began to have money troubles. "What will I do if I can't find a job?" he'd ask his brother, sobbing. On March 19, six months after the economic collapse and a week and a half after the Dow fell below 6,600 . . . Steven Schnipper, 56, was found dead in his apartment. The medical examiner ruled suicide from an overdose of antidepressants. . . . There was no note, just a list of his relatives left on the living room table. "Until now," said his brother, "Steven never caused anyone any trouble."

By committing suicide, Steven Schnipper was causing his brother, Scott, trouble. The solution? The coroner was wrong: Steven Schnipper did not kill himself. Depression killed him:

"People lose jobs all the time and don't kill themselves. Why Steven Schnipper?" Winerip asks rhetorically. Winerip has no interest in learning more about the human dimensions of this particular tragic life. He knows the answer to the question he asked: depression.

Scott, who's now 51 and an editor at Bloomberg News, said he knew that Steven was depressed and was seeing a therapist, but didn't understand he suffered major depression. "I think it was masked by his work and income and the prestige of the jobs at the cosmetics companies. This stripped away his protective layer." . . . Scott Schnipper, who lives in Brooklyn, last saw his brother in February. He suggested an outing to the Brooklyn Botanic Garden and brought along his son Adam, 4, to cheer up Uncle Steven. A mistake. "I was pulled between trying to care for Steven and trying to shield Adam from his distraught uncle," Scott said. He tried to tell his brother he had options. He could sell the condo at a profit, move to a less-expensive area. . . . [T]heir father in Glendale, California had offered spare rooms and even a garage apartment. . . . Scott believes that living in the heart of Manhattan's gay community had become so central to Steven, leaving was unacceptable. . . . Steven had a strong sense of privacy, so it was hard to know how much to intrude. At the memorial service in May, attended by 100 friends and family, people blamed themselves for not intruding more. . . . For a while they worried how to explain the suicide to Adam, but then they decided the easiest way was to tell him the truth: *Uncle Steven died of a disease called depression.*

Such misrepresentation of elementary biology and trivialization of personal tragedy now pass for, and are praised as, compassionate medical reporting and mental health education.

9

One of the most effective methods for confusing the public about the debate concerning voluntary death is to conflate killing oneself (autohomicide) with being killed by or killing another person (heterohomicide) and calling the latter "assisted suicide." Good, bad, or indifferent, killing another person is not the same as killing oneself, as the following vignette illustrates.

Professor Chris Woodhead is a former chief inspector of schools in Britain, widely known there as an outspoken critic of the left-wing education establishment, and the head of Europe's biggest chain of private schools. Afflicted with amyotrophic lateral sclerosis, in May 2009 he told Graeme Paton, education editor for the *Telegraph*, that he will commit suicide rather than die slowly from the disease: "I am clear in my own mind that it is better to end it than continue a life that is extremely frustrating for me and onerous to others who are involved with me. . . . The truth is that I would be more likely to drive myself in a wheel-chair off a cliff in Cornwall than go to Dignitas [the suicide clinic in Zurich, Switzerland] and speak to a bearded social worker about my future."[29]

Although Woodhead goes out of his way to emphasize his rejection of assisted suicide, Paton begins by remarking, "The comments will fuel the debate over the law surrounding assisted suicide. . . . In Britain, it is illegal to assist people to die and legal challenges have failed."

Woodhead's comments did indeed stimulate a lively exchange. Theo Hobson—a well-known British theologian and frequent commentator on religion and public policy—objected to Woodhead's message, declaring that "suicide should remain taboo." However, Hobson—as befits a modern leftist British theologian—equivocates his way out of whatever position he seems to support. He writes:

> I have no idea how keenly I would cling to life in the midst of escalating pain, but I would want to know that the option for a speedy exit was there. A law that shuts off this exit seems inhumane—and the religious believers who preach against assisted suicide seem legalistic, more interested in displaying their brave attachment to principle than in alleviating suffering. And yet a bit of me admits that they have a point. Maybe a slippery slope would be established if it became legal to help a terminally ill, or seriously disabled, person to die. Maybe there would be a cultural shift. . . . Maybe easier assisted suicide would nudge such families into choosing against this difficult but life-affirming course of action. Maybe a taboo against assisted dying is necessary, so that families do their utmost to care for their suffering members, so that the weakest bodies are valued as much as the healthiest. . . . I think there ought to be a culture of disapproval at suicide. . . . *A taboo against suicide is a social necessity, like the incest taboo.* It is a way of affirming life, to say that it is too precious to be thrown away even in the midst of intense suffering. The question is, should this taboo have the weight of the law behind it? The issue is related to abortion, in the sense that this is another taboo that used to be backed up by law. When the law was reformed, the taboo began to weaken. Ideally we would have a stronger taboo against abortion, but retain a humane law.[30]

Hobson basks in the glory of his impractical and insipid proposal to separate taboo and law. Anonymous readers put him in his place:

> You suggest that suicide should remain a taboo but propose no rationale for the statement. . . . [I]f you're going to propose the motion prepare your ground and argument. . . .
>
> Taboo's [sic] are the tools of people who are afraid to face things. The reality is that there are people who want to die and have reasonable grounds for that desire, irrespective of other people's opinion. You do not address the issue by treating people like idiots and maintaining socially sanctioned guilt. You address it through education, understanding and support; giving people as much as society can give in support of their life and understanding and supporting when, despite that, they still make the choice that is theirs to make. I find your position cowardly. . . .
>
> None of us had a choice about coming into this world but we should have the options of how we would like to leave it. For myself I would rather leave it in dignity at a time of my choosing rather than screaming in agony in my own feces, neglected by an understaffed, underfunded and overworked NHS [National Health Service]!

10

Regulating how and when we may kill ourselves is an idea that never occurred even to the most power-mad despots of the ancient world. It has occurred to modern medical despots. None have embraced it more zealously or carried it to such extremes as American psychiatrists, and no people have supported psychiatric despotism as enthusiastically as have the American people.

Modern American society erects many barriers against suicide: it stigmatizes the act, the actor, and often his survivors as well; punishes the attempted or failed suicide by depriving him of liberty; and often holds third parties civilly or criminally responsible for failing to prevent the actor's self-destruction.

Paradoxically, psychiatrists—more than other medical specialists—emphasize the importance of having confidential, trusting relations with patients. Yet psychiatrists—more than other doctors—do not trust their patients and are not trusted by them. This irony is inherent in the psychiatrist's duty to deprive certain individuals of liberty and their privilege to testify in court, as medical experts, that certain individuals are not responsible for their actions.

American psychiatry's founding father, Benjamin Rush, was a medical despot of the first rank. He maintained, "The extensive influence which these opinions [excess of the passion for liberty] had upon the understandings, passions, and morals of many of the citizens of the United States, constituted a form of insanity," and proposed, "Were we to live our lives over again and engage in the same benevolent enterprise, our means should not be reasoning but bleeding, purging, low diet, and the tranquilizing chair."[31]

Anticipating modern psychiatric thinking, Rush declared that certain socially stigmatized behaviors are brain diseases that manifest as insanity and deprive the patient of responsibility for his behavior: "Suicide is madness. . . . Chagrin, shame, fear, terror, anger, unfit for legal acts."[32]

All this now passes as "social science." Matthew Bowker, professor of social sciences at Medaille College in Buffalo, New York, asserts:

> Hostility often masks fear, especially when that hostility is directed against expressions of care. The vitriol we have seen in opposition to the health care bill, which recently included racist and homophobic remarks directed at members of Congress, represents a kind of fearful opposition to the idea of caring for

one another. In America, part of our national story is that we are rugged individualists, pioneers who do not need help or care from anyone. This long-standing mythology becomes . . . dangerous. . . . We depend on government to keep our food and water clean, to catch criminals, to distribute resources, to defend us from enemies and to protect our rights.

Bowker laments that when we "receive care," we feel dependent and vulnerable, as if this were an irrational fear:

It is important to see that this strategy [struggling for independence] is also based on damaged trust and the irrational belief that dependence always results in abuse. . . . Our staunch defense of independence, then, is both honorable and fearful: honorable because in it we take full responsibility for ourselves, fearful because we are afraid of the vulnerability that dependence implies. The exaggerated concern that the health care bill will transform America into a socialist state expresses people's fear of a society of care where no one really cares, where our last defense against painful vulnerability (our independence) is eroded.[33]

In short, rejection of dependence on the government is a symptom of paranoid anxiety, a mental illness.

11

Lawmakers regularly fail to consider the so-called unintended consequences of the coercive policies they propose. This failure is especially important in relation to the prohibition of behaviors people regard as their "natural rights," such as conduct relating to eating, speaking, sex, and drug use. Although Newton's third law of motion is a physical law, it is pertinent to human relations. It states that "in every interaction, there is a pair of forces acting on the two interacting objects. The size of the force on the first object equals the size of the force on the second object. The direction of the force on the first object is opposite to the direction of the force on the second object. Forces always come in pairs—equal and opposite action-reaction force pairs."[34]

An interesting illustration of the operation of this law in relation to suicide prohibition is the formation of a group that calls itself "the Church of Euthanasia" (CoE). Founded by the "Reverend" Chris Korda—son of author and publisher Michael Korda and nephew of famous Hungarian British movie mogul Sir Alexander Korda—the CoE identifies itself as

> a non-profit educational foundation devoted to restoring balance between Humans and the remaining species on Earth. The CoE uses sermons, music, culture jamming, publicity stunts and direct action combined with an underlying sense of satire and black humor to highlight Earth's unsustainable population. According to the church's website, the one commandment is "Thou shalt not procreate." The CoE further asserts four principal pillars: suicide, abortion, cannibalism ("strictly limited to consumption of the already dead"), and sodomy ("any sexual act not intended for procreation"). The church stresses population reduction by voluntary means only. Therefore murder and involuntary sterilization are strictly forbidden by church doctrine. Slogans employed by the group include "Save the Planet, Kill Yourself" . . . and "Eat a Queer Fetus for Jesus," all of which are intended to mix inflammatory issues to unnerve those who oppose abortion and homosexuality. . . . Korda described the project as reflecting his "contempt for and frustration with the profound ugliness of the modern industrial world."[35]

The absurdity of this counterforce to suicide prohibition matches and mirrors the absurdity of the policy that engenders it, though that point is not immediately obvious because the initiatory force enjoys the advantages of seemingly serving an undoubted social good.

Physicians deserve to be lauded for saving the lives of individuals who want to live. Equally, they deserve to be loathed for depriving individuals who want to stop living of the liberty to end their lives.

2

The Suicide Prohibition Agent

1

Medicine is often called a "helping profession." On the commonly held understanding that "help" means aiding an individual advance his own interests, as he sees them, helping a person who wants to kill himself would be like helping a person to read, write, or cook. However, helping a person commit suicide is a criminal act.

Physicians who deprive individuals of the freedom to kill themselves call what they do "suicide prevention." Regardless of what they actually do, physicians like to define themselves as helpers and like to be so defined by the society they serve. Physicians who deprive individuals of the freedom to ingest drugs call what they do "drug abuse prevention and treatment."[1]

Rarely, a physician acknowledges that what he or she actually does and loves to do is exercise power over powerless persons. Julie Holland, MD, writes: "So why am I so attracted to this [emergency room] patient population? I've always been enthralled by insanity. . . . [N]ow I am the doctor in charge of Bellevue's psychiatric emergency room, also known as CPEP (pronounced 'See-Pep,' the Comprehensive Psychiatric Emergency Program). I run two fifteen-hour overnight shifts on Saturday and Sunday nights. They call me 'the weekend attending.' It feels just like rock-and-roll psychiatry to me. This is my Saturday night gig."[2]

Holland's self-portrait of the ER psychiatrist is devastatingly self-incriminating. The police deliver a "patient," a prisoner receiving methadone detoxification. Holland writes:

> "If you are going to release him to me, can you please medicate the hell out of him," the cop finally asks me. I reply as I often do, "Happy and compliant or dead weight?" The cop answers wearily, but without skipping a beat, "If this guy isn't dead weight, I'm afraid I'm going to have to kill him." . . . I go inside to talk to Nancy [the nurse]. "The cop wants dead weight, the prisoner wants methadone. Looks like we should probably just take advantage of the situation." We agree to do something that everyone knows damn well is completely against the rules. I have never done it before or since: I tell the patient we are going to give him an injection of methadone, and we give him Thorazine.
>
> I tell the medical student, "This is the first time in my seven years that I am ever doing this. It's medically unethical what we are doing, do you understand? You never lie to a patient about what medicine they are getting: it's against the rules. Actually, I'm pretty sure it's against the law. But sometimes down here, the end justifies the means. This way, he calms down, the cop is happy, they both leave and we can go on with our night." . . . The medical student nods earnestly. She understands; she doesn't see any problem with what we are doing. She'll make a good ER doc some day, and I tell her so.[3]

Paul R. Linde, an ER psychiatrist in San Francisco, recognizes that implementing legally mandated prohibitions resembles law enforcement more than medical treatment. Most doctors avoid such work. Many seek it. Linde explains why: "I'm a doctor in the psych emergency room at San Francisco General Hospital. . . . One reason I work there is that when I'm not there, I'm not there."[4]

What is ER psychiatry? The Web site of the American Association for Emergency Psychiatry states, "As of 2000, the World

Health Organization estimated one million suicides each year in the world. . . . Conditions requiring psychiatric interventions may include attempted suicide. . . . Emergency psychiatry exists to identify and/or treat these symptoms and psychiatric conditions. . . . A physician's ability to identify and intervene with these and other medical conditions is critical. . . . Mental health professionals in these settings are expected to predict acts of violence patients may commit against themselves (or others)."[5] Attempted suicide, an act, is here transformed into a "symptom" and a "psychiatric condition."

Feeling a need to justify himself, Linde quotes R. D. Laing's granting him and his colleagues absolution: "R. D. Laing has this to say about the potentially coercive power invested in psychiatrists by society: 'We should not blame psychiatrists because we give them such depth of power.'"[6] I do not regard Laing as a moral authority with power to absolve sinners of their sinful behavior—which, moreover, they have no intention to relinquish and is the means by which they support themselves. If we disapprove of medical-psychiatric coercion—as Laing did not but I do—then we *must* blame psychiatrists for eagerly catering to the base human propensity to exploit others.

In contrast to Laing's and Linde's apologetics for coercive psychiatric suicide prevention, Eugen Bleuler (1857–1939) lamented:

> The most serious of all schizophrenic symptoms is the suicidal drive. I am even taking this opportunity to state clearly that our present-day social system demands a great, and entirely inappropriate, cruelty from the psychiatrist in this respect. People are being forced to continue to live a life that has become unbearable for them for valid reasons. This alone is bad enough. However, it is even worse, when life is made increasingly intolerable for these patients. . . . [O]ur worst restraining measures would be unnecessary, if we were not duty-bound to preserve

the patients' lives which, for them as well as for others, are only of negative value. If all this would, at least, serve some purpose! . . . Only in exceptional cases would any of our patients commit suicide, if they were permitted to do as they wished. And even if a few more killed themselves, does this reason justify the fact that we torture hundreds of patients and aggravate their disease? At the present time, we psychiatrists are burdened with the tragic responsibility of obeying the cruel views of society; but it is our responsibility to do our utmost to bring about a change in these views in the near future.[7]

It would be a serious mistake to interpret this passage, written in 1911, as endorsing the view that psychiatrists devalue individuals diagnosed with schizophrenia as having "lives not worth living." To the contrary, Bleuler—an exceptionally fine person and compassionate physician—was pleading for the recognition of the rights of "schizophrenics" to define and control their own lives and that psychiatrists not deprive them of their liberty to take their own lives.

Notwithstanding Bleuler's vast, worldwide influence on psychiatry, psychiatrists ignored his plea to resist "obeying the cruel views of society." On the contrary, Bleuler's invention of schizophrenia lent impetus to the medicalization of the longing for nonexistence, led to the creation of the pseudoscience of "suicidology," and landed psychiatry in the moral morass in which it now finds itself.

2

Linde and his fellow ER psychiatrists believe that their work has special moral merit because they "help people who have been left behind and forgotten by society."[8] This view is a false and selfserving generalization. The young man who "had just had his stomach pumped after downing a hundred ibuprofen and untold quantities of alcohol," cited by Linde, had not been left behind and forgotten by society. Linde accepted his promise that he would not try to kill himself again. Linde released him. "Three days later, the patient hanged himself."[9] Linde then emphasizes the obvious: "that it's still nearly impossible to predict suicides, assaults, or homicides—legal opinions notwithstanding."[10] Perhaps that makes the job, for Linde at least, that much more challenging. Moreover, as everyone knows, committing suicide has little to do with being "left behind and forgotten by society." James Forrestal, Marilyn Monroe, Ernest Hemingway, and countless other famous, successful, wealthy, and well-cared-for persons have died by suicide.

The chapter titles in Linde's book indicate that he recognizes that his job is medical in name only, but he does not let this spoil his fun: "The ER Doc: Who's Calling the Shots?" "The Jailer: If You Want to Go, You Have to Stay," "The Jury: Playing the Suicide Card," and "The Judge: Playing God from a Psychiatric Standpoint."

The practice of coercive suicide prevention rests on the legality and conventional acceptability of imprisoning innocent individuals, called "civil commitment." The ER psychiatrist is a "selection agent": he decides who ought to be deprived of liberty. Linde explains, "Almost all of the twenty patients (an average case load) are in PES [Psychiatric Emergency Services] on an involuntary basis. The State of California's Welfare and Institutions Code 5150 provides the legal justification for a person to be involuntarily taken into custody for up to seventy-two hours for an evaluation on the basis of being a danger to self, danger to others, and/or gravely disabled on the basis of a psychiatric illness. . . . [Psychiatrists are] tasked with deciding whether patients should be retained or released."[11]

Code 5150 does not specify that the jailer be a psychiatrist: it allows a qualified officer or clinician to involuntarily confine a person deemed to have a mental disorder that makes the person a danger to him- or herself, and/or others, and/or gravely disabled. A qualified officer, which includes any California peace officer, as well as any specifically designated county clinician, can request the confinement after signing a written declaration. When used as a term, *5150* (pronounced "fifty-one fifty") can informally refer to the person being confined or to the declaration itself.[12] Implementing the law permitting a physician to act as jailer (gaoler in the United Kingdom) for individuals deemed to be "suicidal" is not the same as seeking and assuming such a role as an occupation and means of earning a living. Obscuring this distinction, suicide prohibition agents like to extol their work as self-sacrificial:

> The PES at San Francisco General is open for business 24 hours a day, 7 days a week, 365 days a year. It is the only designated receiving facility in the city for people placed on 5150 psychiatric holds. Often, working in PES can be compared to diving into the swirl of a cyclone and hanging on for dear life. The staff adjusts to the velocity and spin enough to manage as many as four equally compelling tasks at the same time. It helps to come equipped with an unusual combination of keen diagnostic skills, a sense of humor, tolerance for ambiguity, and the ability to react quickly to changing circumstances.[13]

That is one way to characterize the requirement for the ER psychiatrist's job. Another way is to see it as requiring disdain for the diagnosed-stigmatized mental patient and comfortable self-righteousness about depriving him of his most precious possession, personal freedom. Linde is not unaware of these issues. In the chapter titled "The Jailer," he writes, "An involuntary patient has no legal recourse when detained under section 5150. . . . As a doctor representing the hospital, I often felt like a jailer."[14] Anyone who deprives another person of liberty is, by definition, a jailer. How Linde *feels* about psychiatric coercion has nothing to do with it.

Recognizing the dependence of suicide prevention and psychiatric ER work on commitment laws, Linde refers to the important 1974 Supreme Court case *O'Connor v. Donaldson*, often used as the legal basis for justifying involuntary mental hospitalization and involuntary treatment.[15] A few comments about this case are in order here.

Kenneth Donaldson's saga began in Syracuse, New York, in 1943, when he cast himself in the role of professional mental patient. My entire book *Psychiatric Slavery* (1977) is devoted to a critical analysis of this scandalous case. Suffice it here to emphasize that Donaldson's first admission was as a voluntary patient. Discharged as suffering from schizophrenia, he made his complaint about his "illness" and psychiatric incarceration his career.

In the 1950s, Donaldson began to write a book "as my only means of exposing the harassment and thus hopefully putting an end to it. Before the book was completed, I went to Florida for a visit with my parents. From there I mailed the manuscript to the *Saturday Evening Post*. . . . Three days later I landed in the 'hole' of the Pinellas County Jail in Clearwater on a writ of Inquisition of Incompetency."[16]

Twenty years later, after his Supreme Court "victory," Donaldson's book was published, as was also an article, evidently commissioned in its wake, titled "Blazing a Trail for Mental Patients Who Want to Get Out: Kenneth Donaldson Tells His Own Story."[17] In both, Donaldson systematically misrepresents his psychiatric history. His last decades-long hospitalization was initiated by his father, who, unhappy that his unemployed son had moved in with him and unable to evict him, petitioned the court to have him committed. Ostensibly, he was confined to receive treatment. "Once in the hospital, Donaldson chose to exercise his right [to reject treatment] as a Christian Scientist. The psychiatrists [in a Florida state hospital] chose to respect his right." For this, the courts punished them.[18]

"The crux of Donaldson's claim was that he was deprived of his 'Constitutional right to treatment.' . . . The judge underscored his acceptance of this right by telling the jury that 'the purpose of involuntary hospitalization is treatment. . . . Without such treatment there is no justification from a constitutional standpoint for continued confinement." *O'Connor v. Donaldson* is pure legal-psychiatric legerdemain. Just as Donaldson had been an unwanted guest in his father's house, he was an unwanted patient at the Chattahoochee State Hospital. Like Donaldson's father, the psychiatrists did not want to be responsible for evicting him, waiting for court authorization to do so. For years Donaldson "had town privileges so that he could go back and forth into Chattahoochee at will. . . . In 1966 Donaldson's daughter came to the hospital and wanted to sign him out. Donaldson refused to see her. 'I explained to my children,' he writes, 'that I am not going to be subjected to indignities ladled out by a bunch of goddammedmammy-jamming honey-dippers. If I gave one inch and let my daughter sign me out, I would lose the whole case against institutional psychiatry [*sic*], for then the doctors could say they had cured me and let me go.'"[19]

Donaldson was not interested in freedom. He was fleeing freedom. In the process, he found a cause, "reforming psychiatry." Reciprocally, reformers found him: his litigation for the "right to treatment" was sponsored and supported by the lobby called the Mental Health Law Project and the American Civil Liberties Union (ACLU), both ardent supporters of what they called the "right to treatment," a term that in practice meant the psychiatrist's duty to impose coercive pseudomedical interventions on individuals who did not want to be mental patients.

3

The ACLU has always supported coercive psychiatry. In the Donaldson case, its support of the abstract principle of the "rights of mental patients" led to the Supreme Court's ruling that "a State cannot constitutionally confine *without more* [*sic*] a nondangerous individual who is capable of surviving safely in freedom by himself or with the help of willing and responsible family members or friends." The phrase "without more" was, of course, interpreted as meaning "without more treatment." This was quickly translated into meaning that individuals incarcerated in mental hospitals have a "right to treatment" for their alleged illness. In practice, the patient's "right to treatment" became the psychiatrist's "right to treat," in short his duty to add pharmacological assault to incarceration as the "medical service" he owes his "patient."[20]

Forty years on, Linde complains that, as a consequence, "psychiatrists were now charged with a duty to maintain public safety, a responsibility more consistent with police powers than with medical ones. . . . [E]volving judicial precedents more or less announced that psychiatrists should be able to foresee 'preventable' acts of suicide or violence. It became our job to somehow keep those people locked up, preventing self-harm and mayhem. I refer to this as the crystal ball standard."[21]

Nevertheless, or because of it, Linde loves ER psychiatry. What does he love about it? Presumably that it pays him handsomely for looking into crystal balls and honoring his confabulations as "expert medical testimony." Linde is doing evil but believes he is doing good. He knows he is controlling his patients-prisoners but tells himself that he is caring for them: "The practice of emergency and acute care psychiatry is more highly influenced today by health-care policy makers, insurance and pharmaceutical companies, regulators, activists, and lawyers than it is by those who actually provide the care—namely, psychiatrists, psychologists, psychiatric nurses, nurse practitioners, social workers, pharmacists, and occupational therapists."[22]

Linde manages to misinterpret—or perhaps deliberately invert—my argument in *The Myth of Mental Illness:* "Classifying psychiatric illnesses as medical problems has accomplished several things, many of them useful. . . . [I]n tandem with judicial precedents that have given psychiatrists the unenviable task of trying to predict dangerousness, the *medicalization of mental illness* has produced a notable unintended consequence. It has helped to create a small but significant class of professional patients who have learned to play the suicide card to obtain services."[23]

Citing a 2008 book by a social worker, Linde continues, "Indeed . . . patienthood would not exist without clinicians who readily view the world through the medical model."[24] I would be pleased to regard these unacknowledged allusions to my work as flattering imitations, abundant in the book, but am unable to do so because Linde, like many psychiatrists, uses the term *medical model*—which I have always shunned—incorrectly, indeed stupidly.

The typical patient seen by the general practitioner and internist is an adult who voluntarily seeks his services and with whom the doctor has a contractual relationship. It is the pediatrician whose typical patient is involuntary: a child brought to him by a parent or parent surrogate, by force if necessary. The physician's relationship with his child patient is based on status, not contract. The contract is between doctor and parent, not between doctor and child, who, by legal definition, is not fit to contract. In *Insanity: The Idea and Its Consequences*, I clearly state that "both psychiatry and antipsychiatry rest on a *coercive pediatric model* characterized by relations of domination and subjection, rather than on a *noncoercive medical model* of respect for persons characterized by relations of mutual cooperation and contract."[25] In short, the model of the typical psychiatric relationship ought to be called "pediatric," not "medical."

Linde recognizes the difference between the sick role and disease as a biological condition, dramatically displayed in *One Flew over the Cuckoo's Nest*. Linde writes about lawbreakers "trying on a 'psych jacket' . . . [that] can generally buy you time in a state hospital instead of the penitentiary; it's not necessarily a nice place, but it's a whole lot safer and more comfortable than the pen. It also might buy you Social Security disability benefits when you get out. . . . Many criminals believe that donning a psych jacket gives them an excuse for criminal acts. Diminished capacity."[26]

Linde is silent about the "capacity" of psychiatrists who regard such individuals as bona fide patients, accept the "diagnoses" that their colleagues have attached to them, and make careers, funded by the federal government, of studying and treating the patients' mythical mental illnesses as real diseases. Linde's is an ugly business.

The conversion of voluntary death from crime against oneself to crime against the other, from self-murder to medical malpractice, has now gone so far as to all but eliminate the notion of justifiable, rational suicide. Virtually every case of suicide is "investigated" as if it were a crime, not by the self-killer but by others who might have "bullied" or otherwise mistreated or neglected him and thus "caused" his death.

In August 2010, Kevin Morrissey, the editor of the prestigious *Virginia Quarterly Review,* committed suicide. The journal shut down, and University of Virginia president Teresa A. Sullivan ordered "a thorough review" of the staff's behavior. According to Maria Morrissey, the dead man's sister, "her brother suffered from depression but was pushed to suicide by 'a very hostile work environment.'" On August 12, in a written statement to the *Chronicle of Higher Education,* "[Ted] Genoways, Morrissey's supervisor, denied that he had mistreated Morrissey. 'His long history of depression caused him trouble throughout his career, leading often to conflicts with his bosses.'"[27] The characters have been cast: Morrissey is a victim and Genoways a quasi defendant or, in police jargon, "a person of interest."

4

Lord Acton's famous dictum "Power corrupts and absolute power tends to corrupt absolutely" now applies to psychiatrists even more than to politicians. The life and work of Viktor Emil Frankl (1905–97), psychiatrist and Holocaust survivor, is a sobering illustration.

Born into a middle-class Viennese Jewish family, Frankl attended the gymnasium, studied medicine at the University of Vienna, and became a psychiatrist who specialized in the involuntary treatment of individuals who tried but failed to kill themselves. In the 1930s, until the *Anschluss* in 1938, he was chief physician at the *Selbstmörderpavillon* (suicide pavilion) in the Vienna General Hospital, where he was said to have treated more than thirty thousand suicidal women.[28] After the *Anschluss*, Frankl was appointed head of the neurological department at the Rothschild Hospital, a Jewish institution taken over by the Nazis, where he continued to devote himself to suicide prevention, pleasing the regime by "saving" fellow Jews so they could be killed in the Nazi euthanasia program. During this time, many of his Jewish colleagues helped their coreligionists by writing prescriptions for barbiturates for them, enabling them to take their own lives before the Nazis did so.

Famous mainly for his best-selling *Man's Search for Meaning* (1946), Frankl's first title for this book was *Trotzdem Ja zum Leben Sagen: Ein Psychologe erlebt das Konzentrationslager* (Despite all one must say yes to life: A psychologist survives the concentration camp), a title borrowed from the *Buchenwaldlied* (Buchenwald song), the prisoners' marching song on their way to work).[29] One of its lines is "Wir wollen trotzdem 'ja' zum leben sagen" (Despite all we want to say "yes" to life). The first English title was *From Death-Camp to Existentialism*. In fact, Frankl journeyed from death camp to religious faith.

In addition to chronicling his experiences as a concentration camp inmate, the book presents a synopsis of Frankl's psychotherapeutic method of "finding meaning in all forms of existence, even the most sordid ones, and thus a reason to continue living."[30] The idea of having reason to discontinue living—that suicide may be a rational choice—has no place in Frankl's existential philosophy or psychiatry.

Deported to Theresienstadt, Frankl set up a *Stosstruppe* (shock troop) that functioned as a suicide intelligence service: "Any expression of a suicidal idea or intention would be immediately reported to Frankl. He would then contact the would-be suicide and seek to dissuade him/her."[31]

When a concentration camp guard mocked Frankl for making a lot of money as a physician, he retorted, "As it happens, I did most of my work for no money at all, in clinics for the poor." In that setting Frankl was free to practice psychiatry with truly breathtaking brutality. At the Rothschild Hospital, he was given opportunity to conduct brain surgeries on suicidal patients. Frankl described these interventions in several publications, first in a short article in 1969 in the now defunct British magazine *Encounter:* "In my department at the Vienna Poliklinik [specializing in suicide prevention], we use drugs, and use electroconvulsive treatment. *I have signed authorizations for lobotomies without having cause to regret it. In a few cases, I have even carried out transorbital lobotomy.* . . . What matters is not the technique or therapeutic approach as such, be it drug treatment or shock treatment, but the spirit in which it is being carried out."[32] Frankl does not even allude to obtaining the patient's informed consent to treatment.

In 1945, Frankl returned to Vienna. Appointed professor of neurology and psychiatry at the university, he was later named Vienna's honorary citizen. His dual postwar role—as victim of Auschwitz eager to reconcile with his victimizers and as pioneering existential logotherapist—benefited from the cold war myth

that Austria was a victim of the Nazis. "In order to create a bul-
wark against the Soviets," notes Pytell, "Austria, western Europe
and America all tacitly agreed to sustain the mendacious view
that Austria was a victim of the Nazis. But the truth that everyone knew, was that Hitler, along with many of the leading Nazis,
came from Austria, and there were over six-hundred thousand
Austrian Nazi party members at the end of the war."[33]

In his autobiography, *Was nicht in meinen Büchern steht* (What
does not appear in my books)—published in English as *Recollections: An Autobiography* (1997)—Frankl claimed that although he
had no training in neurosurgery, he found himself nevertheless
able to conduct the surgery:

> When, in order to avoid deportation to concentration camps,
> patients had overdosed on sleeping pills and subsequently had
> been given up for dead by other doctors, Frankl felt justified
> in attempting relatively novel brain surgery techniques. First,
> "some injections intravenously . . . and if this didn't work I gave
> them injections into the brain . . . into the Cisterna Magna. And
> if that did not work I made a trepanation, opened the skull
> . . . inserted drugs into the ventricle and made a drainage so
> the drug went into the Aquaeductus Sylvii. . . . People whose
> breathing had stopped suddenly started breathing again." But
> he could only keep them alive for twenty-four hours, no lon-
> ger. Frankl's drugs of choice were the amphetamines Pervitin
> [methamphetamine] and Tetrophan [a derivative of acridine,
> with no known medical use or value].[34]

5

Part 1 of *Man's Search for Meaning* is titled "Experiences in a Concentration Camp." The conclusion Frankl draws from his experiences is as follows: "From all this we may learn that there are two
races of men in this world, but only these two—the 'race' of the

decent man and the 'race' of the indecent man. Both are found everywhere. . . . No group consists entirely of decent or indecent people." No mention of Jews or Nazis! The book served—perhaps was intended to serve—as a "visa," letting Frankl, the "good Jew," to reenter unrepentantly anti-Semitic postwar Austrian society and be embraced by it: "In spite of all the enforced physical and mental primitiveness of life in a concentration camp, it was possible for spiritual life to deepen. . . . As the inner life of the prisoner tended to become more intense, he also experienced the beauty of art and nature as never before. . . . Yet it is possible to practice the art of living even in a concentration camp, although suffering is omnipresent. . . . Suffering had become a task on which we did not want to turn our backs. We had realized its hidden opportunities for achievement."[35] This formulation effectively robs the concentration camp prisoner of the status of emblematic victim of Nazi depravity.

The Nazi attitude toward Jewish suicide exemplified the political philosophy of the Therapeutic State: everyone, Jews included, is the property of the state; only the state has the right to deliberately destroy human life.[36] Frankl knew this: "The Nazis sought to prevent Jewish suicides. Wherever Jews tried to kill themselves—in their homes, in hospitals, on the deportation trains, in the concentration camps—the Nazi authorities would invariably intervene in order to save the Jews' lives, wait for them to recover, and then send them to their prescribed deaths."[37]

Holocaust scholar Lawrence Langer rightly remarks, "The real hero of *Man's Search for Meaning* was not man but Viktor Frankl." Frankl distorted the reality of Auschwitz in an attempt to prove his own psychophilosophical theories and, in the process, sanctify himself and "blame the victim" who fails to make his concentration camp experience meaningful: "Any man can, even under such circumstances, decide what shall become of him—mentally and spiritually. . . . [I]nner freedom cannot be lost."[38]

Frankl extols the concentration camp experience as an opportunity for the prisoner's moral self-improvement and spiritual purification. Shamefully, years later he even declared, "I do pity those younger people who did not know the camps or live during the war."[39]

Reflecting on the pervasively Christian vocabulary in Frankl's testimony, Langer suggests that "Frankl secretly yearned for a transfiguration of Auschwitz into nothing more than a test of the religious sensibility." Frankl's writings support this interpretation: "Once those people—including my own mother by the way—had been crammed into gas chambers and they saw the canisters of Zyklon B gas thrown into a crowd of naked people, they saw there was no help. Then they began to pray, saying the Shema Israel, and surrendered themselves to what God had bestowed on them—the Communists singing the 'Marseillaise,' the Christians saying the Our Father, the Jews saying Kaddish upon each other."[40] Frankl was not there. He could not have witnessed such a scene. Pytell suggests that Frankl painted this picture to bolster his narrative about suicide and the concentration camp experience:

In using a concentration camp as "punishment" for those who chose suicide rather than capitulation to the Nazis, Frankl appears to suggest that they were cowards and that their deaths serve as examples of the wrong way to die. But by criminalizing the suicidal, Frankl could justify his own experimental research at Rothschild Hospital. The "lesson" also placed Frankl as a moral philosopher in the company of Socrates, Spinoza, and Kant. Yet Frankl's "ascension" came at the expense of the dignity of those who refused to become pawns for the Nazis, and belittled incomprehensible human tragedy. . . . Insofar as his claims portray the Holocaust as a "manageable" experience that (with luck) was survivable, Frankl's version clashes with what we know about the reality of the camps. To understand why Frankl viewed survival in these terms, we must reflect

upon his character, his activities before 1942, his camp experience, and his subsequent intellectual production.[41]

Langer criticizes Frankl's prescription for dying in Auschwitz
as "almost sinister . . . [and] questioned how entering a gas cham-
ber could 'represent a hidden opportunity.' How could one 'suffer
proudly' and 'know how to die' while being asphyxiated?"[42]

Frankl's account of life in the camp is obscene. His amor-
phous-amoral focus on "meaning" is of a piece with his obsession
with sadistic suicide prevention: he celebrates the concentration
camp for allowing Jews to find meaning in "spiritual freedom,"
ignoring that it also allowed Nazis to find meaning in making the
world free of Jews. As Langer notes, "So nonsensically unspecific
is this universal principle of being that one can imagine Hein-
rich Himmler announcing it to his SS men, or Joseph Goebbels
sardonically applying it to the genocide of the Jews! . . . If this
doctrine had been more succinctly worded, the Nazis might have
substituted it for the cruel mockery of *Arbeit Macht Frei*."[43]

6

Before concluding this chapter, I want to contrast the views of
the conventional suicide prohibition agent with the views of an
articulate modern critic of psychiatric suicide prevention.

Hans Maier (1912–78), later Jean Améry, was an Austrian
Holocaust survivor. The similarities between him and Viktor
Frankl end there. Maier's mother was a devout Roman Catholic
innkeeper in the Vorarlberg, the westernmost state in Austria,
who raised her only child in her Catholic faith. His father was
of Jewish descent, long estranged from his faith. "The picture
of him," recalled Améry, "did not show me a bearded sage, but
rather a Tyrolean Imperial Rifleman in the First World War," in
which he was killed.[44]

Maier attended the University of Vienna to study literature and philosophy. In 1933, when Hitler assumed power in Germany, Maier was twenty-one years old, a crucial age especially for a philosophically inclined youth. Educated in the humanities but devoid of professional qualifications, practical skills, and religious identity, he seized on the rise of Nazism to construct an identity for himself in opposition to it: "I wanted by all means to be an anti-Nazi, that most certainly, but of my own accord; I was not yet ready to take Jewish destiny upon myself. . . . I was an Austrian who had been raised as a Christian, and yet I was not one. . . . With Jews as Jews I share practically nothing: no language, no cultural tradition, no childhood memories. . . . The synagogue was the Other."[45]

Was Maier a Jew? The identification of an individual as a member of one or another group, nationality, or race depends on the interests and power of the definer. As a minority group in anti-Semitic Christian Europe, Jews were defined by the majority as the Other, an identification they often embraced or at least accepted. According to Jewish rabbinic law, Maier was not a Jew because his mother was not one. According to German National Socialist law, he was a Jew because his father had been one. Maier resolved this contradiction by formulating his own halachically contrarian definition: he chose to be a Jewish non-Jew—Jean Améry, a German writer who refuses to have his writings published in Germany and Austria.

After the *Anschluss*, Maier married a Jewish woman, more as affirmation of his Jewish self-identification than out of love or wanting a family, much against his mother's objections.

The newlyweds fled to France and then to Belgium. Arrested by the Belgians as a German alien, he was deported to France and wound up interned in the South. He escaped, returned to Belgium, joined the Resistance movement, and was captured by the Nazis, tortured, and shipped to Auschwitz. He survived internments in Auschwitz and Buchenwald and was liberated at Bergen-Belsen in 1945. Only after his release did Maier learn that his mother died of old age, in 1939, unmolested by the Nazis, and that his wife died in 1944, of a heart ailment.

If Viktor Frankl personified the patriotic burgher and *gemütlich* Jew, eager to forgive the Nazis and rejoin his *Bruderschaft*, Maier/Améry personified the disagreeable half-Jew, Christian-born atheist and unforgiving anti-Nazi. In 1955, Maier, aged forty-three, formally changed his name to Jean Améry, a French anagram of his family name. The new name was intended to underscore and symbolize his alliance with French culture and "Frenchness."

For two decades, Améry did not write of his experiences in the death camps. In 1966, when he was fifty-four years old, a fellow German writer urged him to publish a collection of his radio talks. Titled *Jenseits von Schuld und Sühne* (Beyond guilt and atonement), it was translated into English as *At the Mind's Limits: Contemplations by a Survivor on Auschwitz and Its Realities.* Améry lived in the German language he loved, while residing in a land where people spoke French and he never felt at home. His life was bleak, and so are his writings. In 1978, while on a lecture tour, he killed himself.

Unlike Hume's philosophical criticism of suicide prohibition, Améry's criticism is literary and political. Without further comment, I cite below some of his most penetrating observations.

The discourse on voluntary death only begins where psychology ends.[46]

⁓

Today it is sociology, psychiatry, and psychology that are the appointed bearers of public order, that deal with voluntary death as one deals with a sickness. . . . Those whom they call potential "self-murderers" must be hindered from constituting themselves in voluntary death.

~

It has, this society, never troubled itself very much about his existence. . . . Not until now, when he wishes to give in to the inclination toward death, when he is no longer willing to offer any resistance to his disgust with being, when dignity and humanity order him to dispose of the matter neatly and to achieve what he one day will have to achieve anyway: to disappear—only now does society behave as if he were its most precious part and surround him with hideous equipment, parading before him the highly repulsive occupational ambition of physicians who can then ascribe his "rescue" to the credit side of their professional account like hunters when they pace off the spot where their game was slaughtered. In their opinion, they have retrieved him from death and they behave like sportsmen who have succeeded in an extraordinary achievement.[47]

~

Homosexuals, men and women, are not put in quarantine until they are "cured." I don't see why the suicidal should remain the last great outsiders.[48]

But there are good reasons that suicidals remain persecuted by psychiatrists, foremost among them that, unlike homosexuals, suicidals cannot organize and denounce their "protectors." As Ronald Bayer noted in his important book on the conflict between homosexuals and psychiatrists, "With a therapeutic vision so dominant a feature of psychiatric thinking, a divergence between the interests of psychiatry and those to whom it sought to minister was almost inconceivable."[49] In relation to the "right to suicide," it still is.

3

The Marriage of Asclepius
and Atropos

1

In Greek mythology, Asclepius is the god of healing, Atropos
the goddess of dying. In politicized American medicine, their
functions are merged. In 2003, the US Department of Health
and Human Services announced its sponsorship of "an array of
science-based suicide prevention initiatives. This article details
the prevention-related agendas and collaborative efforts of five
operating divisions within the Department of Health and Human
Services: the Substance Abuse and Mental Health Services
Administration, National Institutes of Health, Centers for Disease Control and Prevention, Indian Health Service, and Health
Resources and Services Administration. The article highlights the
Department's activities and their link to the National Strategy for
Suicide Prevention, the plan which will guide the nation's suicide
prevention efforts for the next decade."[1]

The claim that incarceration in the name of suicide prevention is a medical treatment is, prima facie, absurd. People do not
pay doctors to deprive them of liberty. Calling the incarceration of
innocent individuals "science based" is beneath contempt.

In the ancient world, when despotism was the political norm,
no tyrant would have dreamed of regulating whether or when an

individual may or may not kill himself. Today in America, such despotism is second nature to psychiatrists. Perhaps this is a legacy of the missionary zeal with which, in earlier days, Americans preached the gospel of liberty.

2

Following Hume, I believe, as I noted earlier, that we have just as much right and responsibility to regulate how we die as we have to regulate how we live. To be sure, rights and responsibilities are not possessions or things that we have or "own" as private persons. They are attributes that characterize *persons in relation to other persons.* Two (or more) persons ("responders") are needed to generate responsibilities. When we hold ourselves responsible for what we have done, we view our Self as both actor-performer and observer-judge.

We do not and must not hold a person responsible, nor must he hold himself responsible, for a natural event or human action over which he has no control. However, we must hold a person responsible, and he should hold himself responsible, for acts that he can, or ought to be able to, control. Prohibiting death control—like prohibiting birth control and other self-regarding behaviors—reduces the individual's opportunities to assume responsibility for these behaviors and makes the person dependent on external controls instead of self-control. Therein lies the most insidious danger of using prohibitions to regulate behaviors that can, in the final analysis, be effectively regulated *only* by internal controls. If young people believe that they cannot, need not, or must not control how they procreate—because assuming such control is sinful or because others will assume responsibility for the consequences of their behavior—then they are likely to create new life irresponsibly. Similarly, if old people believe that they cannot, need not, or must not control how they die—because assuming such control signifies that they are insane or because others will assume responsibility for the consequences of their behavior—then they are likely to die irresponsibly.

This is not to say that we have a responsibility to commit suicide when, for example, we are a burden to the people around us. Nor does it mean that we have a right to suicide, except in the sense that agents of the state ought to be prohibited from forcibly preventing suicide. I am not praising or condemning, encouraging or discouraging, suicide in the abstract. I merely note that we can choose to live until death claims us or quit life before it does and that this choice and responsibility are similar to our choice and responsibility for, say, staying single or getting married and many similar alternatives. I believe it behooves us to debate and resolve the problem of physician-prevented suicide before we legislate about "physician-assisted" suicide (which easily turns into "physician-provided" suicide, a euphemism for killing or murder by doctors).

Supporters and opponents of the "right to treatment," the "right to die," the "right to physician-assisted suicide," and similarly sloganized "rights" do not limit themselves to arguing their cause. They also litigate in the courts and lobby politicians to impose their preferences on others, using the power of the therapeutic state. Some advocate suicide prevention and prohibition, others suicide provision and assistance. Both groups insist that these practices constitute "medical care" and "help desperately ill patients." I reject the assumptions, rhetoric, and tactics of suicide preventers and suicide providers alike. Suicide is goal-directed behavior for which the actor has reasons and for which he, and he alone, is responsible. Medical considerations are as irrelevant to killing oneself as they are to killing others.

Once an individual enters into a professional relationship with a psychiatrist, he becomes, de facto as well as de jure, a patient and ceases to be a person: qua "mental patient," such a person forfeits his right of self-ownership, and the psychiatrist acquires the duty of protecting him from himself and others from him. Should the psychiatrist deem the "patient" dangerous to himself or others, the psychiatrist is professionally obligated to initiate violence against him, called "civil commitment." If the psychiatrist fails to do so and the patient injures or kills himself or others, the psychiatrist can expect to be the defendant in a tort action for medical negligence—"failure to prevent harm to self or others."

There is no evidence that suicide prevention prevents suicide. Psychiatrists and psychiatric hospitals are regularly sued and found liable for patient suicides. Psychiatrists kill themselves at three times the rate of the general public. Given these facts, it is important that psychiatrists willingly assume—indeed, eagerly seek to shoulder—the risk. In fact, from its beginnings as mad-doctoring, psychiatry was synonymous with the control of the madman by the madhouse keeper. It still is, with the difference that, today, all mental health professionals, in- and outside of mental institutions, are responsible for saving mental patients from themselves. Understanding this arrangement requires familiarity with the historical progress of human relations in Western societies *from status to contract.*

3

In the past, social relations were largely regulated by status. Today, in advanced societies, they are regulated mainly by contract. In liberal (free) societies, the law treats persons as contracting individuals, not as members of status groups (male or female, black or white).

I have presented the history of "mad-doctoring"—later promoted to real doctoring and renamed "psychiatry"—elsewhere. In the nineteenth century, the state mental hospital system was the pride of the nation.[2] In the mid-twentieth century, after the

Second World War, the system became the "shame of the nation."[3] Over this long period and since then, the coercive, pseudomedical ideology of psychiatry undermined traditional ideas of personal responsibility and eroded constitutional limits on the role of the federal government. This transformation is dramatically illustrated by a comparison of the views of President Franklin Pierce (1804–69) and President John Kennedy (1917–63) concerning the role of the federal government in providing services for the mentally ill.

Before the Civil War, psychiatric dogma held that insanity is an easily curable disease, provided that the "sufferer" is incarcerated in an insane asylum "early," that is, soon after the onset of his "illness." Dr. William M. Awl, superintendent of the Ohio State Lunatic Hospital in Columbus, recorded in his annual report for 1843: "Per cent of recoveries on all recent cases discharged the present year, 100." Other asylum directors claimed to have achieved similar results. "The records of this Asylum," stated Dr. Luther V. Bell, head of the McLean Asylum in Cambridge, "justify the declaration that all cases, certainly recent . . . recover under a fair trial. This is the general law." Dr. Thomas S. Kirkbride, superintendent of the Pennsylvania Hospital for the Insane, asserted, "The general proposition that truly recent cases of insanity are commonly very curable . . . may be considered as fully established."[4]

The result of these "psychiatric reforms" was triumph for the mad-doctor, and tragedy for the madman. In principle, the insane-asylum inmate was restored to full citizenship. In practice, he became a nonperson: a "ward of the state," in the words of social reformer Horace Mann (1796–1859).[5] The alienist's claim that insanity was an easily curable disease laid the ground for the division of modern secular societies into two classes of citizens, sane and insane, persons unmolested by psychiatrists and individuals enslaved by them.

Dorothea Lynde Dix (1802–87), an energetic New Englander, found mental health care—not yet so called—the ideal arena in which to exercise her ambition to do good. She dedicated herself to establishing psychiatric plantations all over the United States. In a relatively short time, she sparked the founding of thirty-two insane asylums and fifteen "schools" for the feebleminded. Dix's reformist zeal meshed with the temper of her times. Growing in numbers and becoming more urbanized, American families and communities wanted to get their troublesome members out of sight and out of mind. Dix offered to satisfy their need and at the same time soothe them with the fiction that her proposed plantations would make the slaves happy and healthy.

In the late 1840s, Congress made generous donations of public land to the states for the advancement of public education and public works. This move inspired Dix to petition Congress for support: "I confide to you the cause and the claims of the destitute and of the desolate, without fear or distrust. I ask, for the thirty states of the Union, 5,000,000 acres of land, of the many hundreds of millions of public lands, appropriated in such manner as shall assure the greatest benefit to all those who are in circumstances of extreme necessity, and who, through the providence of God, are wards of the nation."[6]

When first introduced, the bill Dix sponsored failed to pass in Congress. Dix persevered and raised her request to more than twelve million acres. In 1854, her bill passed both houses but was vetoed by President Franklin Pierce. The text of his veto is relevant to our present medical-political-economic situation.

One need not be a constitutional scholar to understand that the founders' "original intent" was to create a *limited federal government,* leaving governance of most day-to-day affairs to the people or the states. Were the federal government to fund and regulate the management of human misery—categorized with grab-bag terms like *destitution* and *insanity*—it would inexorably exercise the kind of power over people against which the founders had fought. This is exactly what has happened. Explained Pierce:

> The bill entitled "An act making a grant of public lands to the several States for the benefit of indigent insane persons," which was presented to me on the 27th ultimo, has been maturely considered, and is returned to the Senate, the House in which it originated, with a statement of the objections which have required me to withhold from it my approval. . . . *It cannot be questioned that if Congress has the power to make provision for the indigent insane without the limits of this District it has the same power to provide for the indigent who are not insane, and thus to transfer to the Federal Government the charge of all the poor in all the States. It has the same power to provide hospitals and other local establishments for the care and cure of every species of human infirmity, and thus to assume all that duty of either public philanthropy or public necessity to the dependent, the orphan, the sick, or the needy which is now discharged by the States themselves or by corporate institutions or private endowments existing under the legislation of the States.* The whole field of public beneficence is thrown open to the care and culture of the Federal Government. Generous impulses no longer encounter the limitations and control of our imperious fundamental law; for however worthy may be the present object in itself, it is only one of a class. It is not exclusively worthy of benevolent regard. Whatever considerations dictate sympathy for this particular object apply in like manner, if not in the same degree, to idiocy, to physical disease, to extreme destitution. If Congress may and ought to provide for any one of these objects, it may and ought to provide for them all. And if it be done in this case, what answer shall be given when Congress shall be called upon, as it doubtless will be, to pursue a similar course of legislation in the others? . . . The decision upon the principle in any one case determines it for the whole class. The question presented, therefore, clearly is upon the constitutionality and propriety of the Federal Government assuming to enter into

a novel and vast field of legislation, namely, that of providing for the care and support of all those among the people of the United States who by any form become fit objects of public philanthropy. I readily and, I trust, feelingly acknowledge the duty incumbent on us all as men and citizens, and as among the highest and holiest of our duties, to provide for those who, in the mysterious order of Providence, are subject to want and to disease of body or mind; but *I can not find any authority in the Constitution for making the Federal Government the great almoner of public charity throughout the United States. To do so would, in my judgement, be contrary to the letter and spirit of the Constitution and subversive of the whole theory upon which the Union of these States is founded.*[7]

4

After the Second World War, politicians and psychiatrists recognized that incarcerating innocent people in state mental hospitals was inimical to the bodily and mental health of the inmates and that the increasing expense of maintaining them was bankrupting the states.[8] Mirabile dictu, at this moment scientists discovered new "miracle drugs" deemed "effective" for mental illnesses. Long-term psychiatric institutionalization was declared unnecessary. Thus was a new golden age of psychiatry born, the era called "deinstitutionalization," ostensibly eliminating the "snake pits" and justifying the federal government's assumption of the duty to care for the mentally ill. The Camelot of Psychiatric Quackery had arrived.

In January 1963, for the first time in history, the president of the United States devoted a part of his State of the Union address to lecturing his audience on mental health. A month later, he delivered a special message to Congress, titled "Mental Illness and Mental Retardation," declaring, "I propose a national mental health program to assist in the inauguration of a wholly new emphasis and approach to the care of the mentally ill. . . . We need . . . to return mental health care to the mainstream of American medicine." Kennedy proposed the establishment of community mental health centers and promised to cure the majority of "schizophrenics."[9]

Subsequent presidents escalated the rhetoric about the magnitude of the problem of mental illness and the successes of its medical solution. In 1999, at a White House conference, President William Clinton declared: "Mental illness can be accurately diagnosed, successfully treated, just as physical illness." Tipper Gore, the president's mental health adviser, emphasized, "One of the most widely believed and most damaging myths is that mental illness is not a physical disease. Nothing could be further from the truth." First Lady Hillary Clinton added, "The amygdala acts as a storehouse of emotional memories. And the memories it stores are especially vivid because they arrive in the amygdala with the neurochemical and hormonal imprint that accompanies stress, anxiety, and other intense excitement. . . . We must . . . begin treating mental illness as the illness it is on a parity with other illnesses."[10]

We have come a long way since Pierce. He saw that if the federal government assumed responsibility for relieving the people of the demands of life, the result would be the destruction of the limited government that was the original raison d'être of the United States of America and the individual liberty it guaranteed. Pierce did not foresee how soon the American people would reject their commitment to local versus central government, how quickly the very term *states' rights* would become a term of disdain and disapprobation.

4

Separation

Emigration, Secession, Suicide

1

Why do people kill themselves? Because they are mentally ill. Death from suicide, experts on mental health insist and the press repeats, is the result of mental illness, just as death from cancer is the result of bodily illness.[1] This is nonsense—mindless belief in a literalized metaphor endowed with the power of agency: "Suicide kills."

According to prevailing psychiatric dogma, answering the question, "Why did X kill himself?" with "Because he wanted to die" is *empirically and statistically* wrong. I believe it is a priori right. Declared famous Roman poet Ovid (Publius Ovidius Naso, 43 BCE–AD 18): "*Spectemur agendo*" (Let us be judged by our acts). Although most people today might say and believe that they agree with that principle, in fact they do not: they do not judge people by their acts; they judge them by the politically correct *interpretation of the meaning* of their acts. Thus, killing oneself does not signify wanting to die. It signifies mental illness, religious fanaticism, sometimes even heroism in an admirable cause. Never a decision to leave life. Thus, when a "researcher" of Islamic suicide bombers "discovers" that his subjects want to kill themselves, his contrarian "findings" are "news." From a 2010 report in the *Boston Globe*, titled "The Truth About Suicide Bombers," we learn:

> Qari Sami [a suicide bomber] was a young man who kept to
> himself, a brooder. He was upset by the US forces' ouster of
> the Taliban in the months following 9/11—but mostly Sami
> was just upset. He took antidepressants daily. One of Sami's
> few friends told the media he was "depressed." . . . Brian Wil-
> liams, associate professor of Islamic studies at the University
> of Massachusetts Dartmouth, was in Afghanistan at the time.
> Williams thinks that "Sami never really cared for martyrdom;
> more likely, he was suicidal." The traditional view of suicide
> bombers is well established, and backed by the scholars who
> study them. . . . But Williams is among a small cadre of scholars
> from across the world pushing the rather contentious idea that
> some suicide bombers may in fact be suicidal.[2]

In the United States, 10.9 out of 100,000 persons die by suicide. For persons between twenty and twenty-four, the figure
is 12.5, and for those persons above sixty-five, it is 14.2. In short,
the persons most likely to kill themselves are the young and
the old. After listing these prevalence rates, the Web site of the
National Institute of Mental Health adds, "A person who appears
suicidal should not be left alone and needs immediate mental-
health treatment. . . . [B]ecause research has shown that mental
and substance-abuse disorders are major risk factors for suicide,
many programs also focus on treating these disorders as well as
addressing suicide risk directly."[3]

Like virtually all so-called mental health information, this
statement is false, intended to distract attention from the reasons
people choose death over life. What are the reasons? Simply put,
escaping a life they view as worse than death. Although each person's reason for killing himself is uniquely personal, we might
say that the young choose voluntary death to escape the pain and
responsibility of having to make a life for themselves, the old to
escape the loss of autonomy owing to age, disease, and disability.

In short, the simplest and most plausible explanation-motive for suicide at any age is the desire to separate oneself from "it," the nature of "it" differing among age groups, socioeconomic classes, cultures, and nations. As always, the actions of the suicide speak louder than the words of the persons who presume to speak for them, while seeking to deprive them of liberty. The suicidal person wants to get away from his life, his social environment. *His action is best viewed as a form of emigration or secession.* As Jean Améry, the Austrian "Jewish" Holocaust survivor and bitter opponent of suicide prevention, put it, "I don't like the word *Selbstmord* (self-murder). . . . I prefer to speak of *Freitod* (voluntary death). . . . [T]here is no carcinoma that devours me, no infarction that fells me, no uremic crisis that takes away my breath. *I* am that which lays hands upon me, who dies after taking barbiturates, 'from hand to mouth.'"[4]

Webster's defines *emigration* as "leav[ing] one's place of residence or country to live elsewhere" and *secession* as "withdrawal into privacy or solitude, retirement; formal withdrawal from an organization." Both terms refer to and are in part synonymous with *separation,* defined as "the act or process of separating: the state of being separated . . . cessation of cohabitation between a married couple by mutual agreement or judicial decree; termination of a contractual relationship (as employment or military service)."

Interpreted as a kind of emigration, the suicide decides to move from the land of the living to the land of the dead. Viewed as a kind of secession, the suicide chooses to firmly separate himself from his family and society.

Every emigrant knows from personal experience that it is painful to leave one's home and exchange one's mother tongue for a "foreign" language. Many people are deeply unhappy with their circumstances in their homeland, but few emigrate even if they have the opportunity to do so.[5] The situation with respect to suicide is similar: many people are deeply dissatisfied with their life, but few choose to leave it. Why? Because of feelings of responsibility for dependents left behind, fear of the unknown, the dread of nonexistence, and many other reasons.

Our sense of existence is intrinsically dialogic. We are social creatures through and through. Strictly speaking, there is no such thing as an independent, self-sufficient, autonomous individual. That fact does not render the term *autonomous* less useful. It requires only that we keep in mind that our need for autonomy is permanently at odds with our need for relationships with other human beings (or imaginary or nonhuman beings endowed with human attributes, such as gods and pets).

This understanding of autonomy requires that we attribute it only to *persons as individuals,* never to persons-in-relation—for example, patients. It is as foolish to talk about "patient autonomy" as it is to talk about "spouse autonomy" or "orchestra player autonomy" or "soccer player autonomy." Each member of such a pair or team willingly enters into a human bond, the very point of which is to relinquish some portion of his autonomy (independence) in exchange for some other goods (such as security or service or team effort). Why else would man create God, if not to love him and be loved by him in return? I suspect that this point is why the gods of the monotheistic religions condemn suicide.

2

The conventional explanation that, in the monotheistic religions, suicide is forbidden by the commandment "Thou shalt not kill"— a mistranslation of "Thou shalt not murder"—is unpersuasive. Other types of killings-murders are permissible, some even praiseworthy. It seems more plausible to interpret the prohibition against suicide as God's commanding man never to abandon him, a directive explicitly stated in the Old Testament: "Thou shalt have no other gods before me" (Exod. 20:3).

Why this demand for exclusivity? The Greeks and Romans had numerous gods who kept each other company. The Jewish God is alone in the world, married to man. His greatest fear is divorce; hence, he prohibits it.

Formerly, we protected ourselves from our fatal freedom by clinging to monotheism, monarchy, and monogamy.[6] Today, we protect ourselves by placing our faith in monomedicine, monoscience, and monogovernment (the total state, the therapeutic state). Each of these arrangements promises to satisfy our craving for security and certainty, conditions absent in real life. Hence the ever-recurring lament of the pious abandoned, "My God, my God, why hast thou forsaken me?" (King David, Psalm 22).

It seems likely that the invention of a god whom we must never abandon and who promises never to abandon us originates from the infant's need never to be separated from his mother. Human life is inherently precarious, and humans *know* it is. The prohibition "You must never leave (me)!" and the promise "I will never leave (you)!"—communications lovers sometimes exchange in precisely those terms—are effective, albeit illusory, protections against this basic anxiety. This point is why autohomicide qua selfish suicide and autohomicide qua selfless self-sacrifice are two sides of the same coin.

If we perceive suicide as a selfish act—the egoistic *detachment* of the self from the Other in the here and now—we interpret it as sinful or sick. On the other hand, if we perceive suicide as the timeless *attachment* of the self to the Other—in the hereafter as in *Romeo and Juliet*, or to God as in martyrdom—we interpret autohomicide as reasonable and admirable.

In the traditional religious worldview, the sole agent with legitimate power to decide who should live and who should die is God, the Creator. In the modern medical view, the sole such agent is the therapeutic state. Secession—defiance of control by church, state, medicine—is the ultimate escape from oppression, the ultimate declaration of freedom.

3

"Secession" is the peaceful (nonviolent), voluntary separation of political entities. Analogically, we may view divorce as marital secession and suicide as personal secession. (The fact that not all those individuals personally affected may find the separation voluntary or peaceful—for example, children in a divorce—is important but does not affect the argument I am advancing.)

As Americans, we tend to associate the term *secession* with the Civil War, slavery, and states' rights. This view is shortsighted. The sole aim of the Revolutionary War (War of Independence) was *secession* from the government of King George III. "Most Americans seem to be unaware that 'Independence Day' was originally intended to be a celebration of the colonists' *secession* from the British empire," writes historian Thomas J. DiLorenzo. "The Revolutionary War was America's first war of secession. . . . The word 'secession' was not a part of the American language at that time, so Jefferson used the word 'separation' instead to describe the intentions of the American colonial secessionists."[7]

From the beginning, there were disagreements among the founders: some wanted to form a powerful centralized state, while others wished to maintain the independence of their respective regions by creating a loose confederation of states. "If any state in the Union will declare that it prefers separation . . . to a continuance in union . . . I have no hesitation in saying, 'let us separate,'" wrote Thomas Jefferson to William H. Crawford, Monroe's secretary of the Treasury, in 1816.[8] In 1862, Abraham Lincoln defended his war on the South with the opposite rationale:

My paramount object in this struggle is to save the Union, and is not either to save or to destroy slavery. If I could save the Union without freeing any slave I would do it, and if I could save it by freeing all the slaves I would do it; and if I could save it by freeing some and leaving others alone I would also do that. What I do about slavery, and the colored race, I do because I believe it helps to save the Union; and what I forbear, I forbear because I do not believe it would help to save the Union.[9]

Consistent with his view on political secession, Jefferson regarded suicide as a rational remedy for personal disaster. In 1779, the Virginia legislature was considering a bill for the repeal of the punishment for suicide. Jefferson supported repeal and offered the following statement on its behalf:

Suicide is by law punishable by forfeiture of chattels. This bill exempts it from forfeiture. The suicide injures the State less than he who leaves it with his effects. If the latter then not be punished, the former should not. As to the example, we need not fear its influence. Men are too much attached to life, to exhibit frequent instances of depriving themselves of it. At any rate, the quasi-punishment of confiscation will not prevent it. For if one can be found who can calmly determine to renounce life, who is so weary of his existence here, as rather to make experiment of what is beyond the grave, can we suppose him, in such a state of mind, susceptible of influence from the losses to his family by confiscation? That men in general, too, disapprove of this severity, is apparent from the constant practice of juries finding the suicide in a state of insanity; because they have no other way of saving the forfeiture. Let it then be done away.[10]

Jefferson's reasoning here echoes David Hume's reasoning in his essay "On Suicide," published two years earlier. Also pertinent to Jefferson's views on suicide is his correspondence with Dr. Samuel Brown, a professor of medicine at the university in Lexington, Virginia, concerning the use of toxic plants for killing oneself. On July 14, 1813, Jefferson wrote to Brown, "The most elegant thing of that kind known is a preparation of the Jamestown weed, *Datura-Stramonium,* invented by the French in the time of Robespierre. Every man of firmness carried it constantly in his pocket to anticipate the guillotine. It brings on the deep sleep as quietly as fatigue does the ordinary sleep, without the least struggle. . . . It seems far preferable to the Venesection of the Romans, the Hemlock of the Greeks, and the Opium of the Turks. . . . There are ills in life as desperate and intolerable, to which it would be the rational relief."[11]

Jefferson is describing, perhaps even recommending, the use of *Datura stramonium* as an herbal medicine useful for suicide. The source of this toxic chemical is the common plant known by many names, among them angel's trumpet, devil's weed, jimsonweed, and Jamestown weed. The term *stramonium* is originally from the Greek *strychnos* (nightshade) and *manikos* (mad). All parts of *Datura* plants contain significant quantities of the alkaloids atropine, hyoscyamine, and scopolamine, chemicals that may be fatal if ingested by humans or animals. In the United States the plant is called "Jamestown weed" after the city in Virginia, where British soldiers were drugged with it while attempting to suppress Bacon's Rebellion in 1676. Today, a person who so casually informs another of the suicidal potential of a readily available substance, as Jefferson did, runs the risk of being charged with the crime of "assisting suicide."

The result of this cultural-legal atmosphere is the destruction of privacy and trust in the helping professions. Suicide prohibitions have not succeeded in preventing suicides but have succeeded in preventing people from having an honest, private conversation about life and death. Those persons who trust mental health professionals with their innermost thoughts may quickly find themselves punished with a "seventy-two-hour hold" or worse. Suicidal persons and their would-be helpers alike are paralyzed by prohibitionist censorship, deception, and legislation requiring the betrayal of trust. The first and major victim of the war on suicide, as in all wars, is loss of liberty.

4

Psychiatrists are expected—legally, medically, socially—to prevent individuals from killing themselves. As professionals, they are also expected to lie and withhold information about the subject and instruct journalists to do the same, all in the name of public health.

In 2009, *Psychiatric News* ran an article titled "Psychiatrists Urged to Work with Journalists on Reporting of Suicides."[12] Medical writer Mark Moran reports that the Canadian Psychiatric Association instructed its members to "educate" journalists about ways of reporting that do not encourage copycat suicides: this was one of the recommendations in a policy paper titled "Media Guidelines for Reporting Suicide," in which the CPA summarized recommendations formulated by the US Centers for Disease Control and Prevention and the Canadian Association for Suicide Prevention for journalists. "Since media often call psychiatrists to comment on suicide," states the paper, "it is crucial for psychiatrists to have this knowledge readily available. These requests can be an opportunity for educating the media and ultimately saving lives." The recommendations include avoiding reporting the following: details of the suicide method, the word *suicide* in the headline, and approval of the suicide. In contrast, the recommendations encourage journalists to convey the following when reporting a suicide: alternatives to suicide (that is, treatment); community resource information for those with suicidal ideation; examples of a positive outcome of a suicidal crisis, such as calling a suicide hotline; warning signs of suicidal behavior; and ways to approach a suicidal person. Similar recommendations have been published by the American Foundation for Suicide Prevention, in collaboration with the American Association of Suicidology, the Centers for Disease Control and Prevention, the National Institute of Mental Health, the Substance Abuse and Mental Health Services Administration, the Office of the Surgeon General, and the Annenberg Public Policy Center. These efforts to transform the media into loyal soldiers in the war on suicide are similar to the efforts that medical politicians used to mobilize the country—indeed the Western world—to fight the war on drugs.

Accordingly, people can no longer trust physicians, teachers, science writers, or journalists, most of whom have been co-opted, suborned, or simply seduced by the antisuicide apparatus of the Mental Health System. If they have lived well or are just lucky, people may be able to trust parents, siblings, adult children, or friends. In their anonymous identity in the protected sphere of the Internet, they can also trust one another to engage in honest dialogue, safe from Big Brother as Grand Therapeutic Inquisitor.

Physicians, especially psychiatrists, have abandoned their traditional roles as trustworthy confidants and counselors of troubled persons, forfeiting their ministerial functions. People seeking to engage in a meaningful conversation about suicide must bypass newspapers, radio, television, and even monitored Web sites and create their own protected sphere. The Usenet newsgroup ASH (ash or a.s.h., alt.suicide.holiday) has provided such a service.[13]

The term *Usenet* refers to an *unmoderated Internet discussion system*. Some newsgroups are moderated, that is, messages submitted by readers are e-mailed to the moderators of the newsgroup, for approval. The job of moderators is to ensure that "messages that the readers see in newsgroups conform to the charter of the newsgroup. Such articles bear the Approved: header line." Messages submitted by readers for unmoderated newsgroups are published for everyone to see.[14]

While ASH's original purpose was to discuss the relationship between suicide rates and holiday seasons, hence its name, it has "evolved into a broad discussion forum where suicidal and depressed people can openly share their thoughts. Some participants are not suicidal, but post to provide psychological support and other input to suicidal or depressed posters. According to its FAQ [frequently asked questions], its purpose is neither to encourage nor discourage suicide."

The community has developed its own unique terminology, revealingly based on the metaphors of travel. Thus, "'Catch the bus' refers to the act of suicide, and the group is described as: 'A bus stop where several people have decided to stop and chat before deciding on whether or not to get on the bus.'" According to the ASH site,

> Because ASH is a non-moderated Usenet newsgroup, it is technically impossible to ban any person from posting to ASH. Because of this, ASH cannot be classified as being pro-choice or pro-life: posters in the newsgroup represent wide range of positions from strict anti-suicide to right-to-die.
>
> ASH is often mistakenly called a website; in fact it is a Usenet newsgroup from the alt.* hierarchy and not a website. This makes a significant legal difference, and allows ASH to exist despite attempts to close suicide websites. Unlike websites, Usenet newsgroups are not regulated by any central authority, and there is no organization or individual responsible for a particular newsgroup. . . . Recent research shows that suicide websites indeed could be more efficient in providing emotional help for people contemplating suicide than suicide hotlines. . . .

> High degree of anonymity is another advantage of newsgroups like ASH, allowing people to openly talk about their feelings without fear of consequences. . . . ASH does not censor information on suicide methods and does not prohibit such discussion. Opponents see discussion of suicide methods as potentially endangering vulnerable people—people who would otherwise live through crisis, might commit suicide given information on lethal methods. Supporters of open discussion state that methods information is widely and legally available; . . . there is no indication that making such information available changed suicide rates.

The passion to control others—manifested, for example, by censoring what people can hear or read or what drugs they may ingest—can be restrained only by self-control. Citing empirical evidence demonstrating the ineffectiveness—or, indeed, the counterproductivity—of certain social practices generated by the passion to control is a notoriously feeble counterpoise against it. The futility of appeals to evidence is illustrated by the fact that even such ostensible opponents of suicide prohibition as Final Exit use medicalized premises, absurdly promoting a "right to suicide" contingent on medical criteria and medical judgment. Under the heading "Our Guiding Principles," the Web site of the organization states: "Mentally competent adults have a basic human right to end their lives when they suffer from a fatal or irreversible illness or intractable pain, when their quality of life is personally unacceptable, and the future holds only hopelessness and misery. . . . We do not encourage anyone to end their life, do not provide the means to do so, and do not actively assist in a person's death. We do, however, support them when medical circumstances warrant their decision."[15] The Bill of Rights presumes that the people to whom it is addressed are mentally competent. There is no mention in that document of "mental competence," a term that implies a "medical" judgment, granted or withheld by psychiatric authority. The fact that today even individuals and organizations that ostensibly condone suicide treat voluntary exit from life as a psychiatrically permitted option, yet call it a "basic human right," illustrates how medically contaminated and morally degraded our concept of human rights has become.

There is only one US Constitution and Bill of Rights. Supporters of the therapeutic state deprive individuals they deem mentally ill of the protections of the Bill of Rights, posit that the protections apply only to the mentally healthy, and occupy themselves with drafting new "Mental Patients' Bills of Rights."

5

Everyone wants to die a "good death." Where people differ is in their understanding of the term. The ancient Greeks viewed a "good death" as the culmination of an "objectively desirable 'good' life," creating eudaimonia, usually translated as "happiness." Such a death was considered a rare and admirable achievement.[16] Today, most people believe that how they die has nothing to do with how they live, that they have a "right" to a good death, defined as a death free of pain and suffering. *Imperfect Endings*, a recent book by Zoe FitzGerald Carter, is an example of the death of such a person.[17]

Ostensibly a tribute to her mother, Mary Curtis Ratcliff (Margaret in the book), *Imperfect Endings* is an overlong lament about her egotism, vanity, and determination to control her children's lives, capped by her plans for killing herself in their presence, her idea of a "perfect death."[18] This was the last thing the daughters— Katherine, Zoe, and Hannah—wanted.

Why does Margaret—seventy-five and generally healthy— want to end her life? Because, she says, she suffers from

Parkinson's disease and does not want to wait until the disease kills her. In fact, she is nowhere near death from Parkinsonism or any other illness. Ostensibly, the three daughters support their mother's decision:[19]

"'You know, Zoe [says Katherine], I do think Momma has the right to die if she wants to.' 'I do too,' I say, wondering if this is true. 'But it's not just a question of rights. It's about whether or not it makes sense.' . . . It made perfect sense to my mother, so who am I talking about? Myself, obviously. And the reason it doesn't make sense to me is that I don't want her to die. Her willingness to consider it makes me feel inconsequential, like I'm not worth sticking around for.'"[20] Margaret—a moneyed member of Washington high society, the widow of an alcoholic, womanizing lawyer—regards herself entitled to a comfortable death. Together with Zoe, they set off on a round of visits to physicians whom they expect to assist them.

"My mother and I went to see Dr. Harmon, a local psychiatrist and prominent member of the Hemlock Society . . . and request a prescription for Seconal." Harmon goes through the ritual mental-status examination required before providing such a medical service. Reassured by both women that the "patient" is not depressed, he says, "You have come to get a prescription for Seconal. Am I right? . . . Good. I'll write it for you and you can get it filled today if you wish. Wait a couple of months and then get it refilled. Your third refill should be two months after that. We don't want to alarm the pharmacist."[21]

Scoring Seconal so easily leaves Margaret and Zoe unsatisfied. After egging on one another with fears that ingesting the drug might fail to be fatal, they contact the local branch of the Hemlock Society and make arrangements to be visited by a suicide counselor. The counselor—whom Margaret and Zoe promptly belittle, dubbing him "Mr. Death"—is a poor naif "from Tulsa, Oklahoma," who asks to be called "Bud": "My mother is a solid Washington

Democrat, a liberal even, but she is also a cultural and intellectual snob, and this man is definitely not a member of the tribe."[22]

Bud ignores the disrespect of his clients and explains that the Hemlock Society offers to supplement Seconal, if necessary, with helium, to asphyxiate the patient: "We stay with her until we're sure she is dead, take the tank and everythin' and leave. Y'all call the coroner's office to let 'em know there's been a death. They show up." Worried about detection and blame, Zoe pesters Bud: "So what if they notice she's has just been suffocated? Or has helium in her system?" "Well, I can tell you, in my experience, that's never happened. . . . I jus' want you folks to know I don't get paid to do this job. I do it 'cause I believe in it."[23]

Worried that Rosa—Margaret's loyal, longtime Chilean Catholic housekeeper—might denounce the daughters for facilitating their mother's suicide, Katherine admonishes Zoe: "You may be willing to play along with her games, but I'm not."[24] Margaret—who has a master's degree in clinical psychology from Columbia University—pleads: "'I was hoping all three of you could be here.' 'Okay, so all three of us will be facing murder charges,' Katherine bellows."[25]

Meanwhile, in San Francisco, Zoe's devoted husband, Jack—in-house counsel for a Silicon Valley high-tech company—grows tired of his wife's limitless willingness to subordinate his needs and the needs of their family to Margaret's vagaries:

"She's toying with you, honey," Jack says in a terse, aggrieved voice the morning after my return. "I doubt she has any intention of killing herself at all. It's just a weird bid for attention. And the worst part is, you keep falling for it. . . . Your mother isn't dying, she's talking about dying, or killing herself, or getting someone else to kill her, or whatever it is this week. And she's got you in a state over it. . . . How long is she going to keep this up? Calling everyone to announce some new plan

every five minutes. . . . How long are you going to run to her
every time she calls? . . . This has been going on for close to a
year. How much longer are you going to put up with it?" I can't
answer that question. No, I can answer that question. . . . I will
always run to her when she calls.[26]

Jack understands what's going on but is too decent to make
Zoe's life even more difficult. Margaret is a spoiled, rich woman,
commanding a stable of doctors who cater to her wish to rotate her
suicide plan. Rejecting both Seconal and suffocation, she reports
to Zoe: "Dr. Fielding had prescribed me morphine. . . . Apparently
it's quite easy to do. And it's unlikely anyone would notice since I'd
be taking it for pain anyway. So I was thinking perhaps morphine
is the way to go." Zoe erupts: "I'm sick of talking about this all the
time. It's all we ever talk about. . . . Do you ever think for one second
that I might be doing something? Like playing with my children?"[27]

Unrepentant, Margaret retaliates: "'Well, it won't be for very
much longer,' my mother says coldly. . . . Doesn't she have some
responsibility to help me process this? Isn't that part of the message in all those books she reads, the Good Death creed she so
ardently subscribes to? . . . 'Don't try to make me feel sorry for
you [Zoe soliloquizes]. Remember, you are not dying—you are
choosing to die.'"[28]

Margaret continues to set new suicide dates and justifies the
extensions by attributing them to her love for her children and
grandchildren: "Don't worry. . . . I am waiting to get copies of
my novel made for the three of you. And then there's that children's story I told you about. Something I want to finish for all the
grandchildren."[29]

And so mother and daughters stumble from one deception
and self-deception to another. Margaret obtains a bottle of liquid
morphine. Zoe's phobic, war-on-drugs mind-set now takes over:
"To me the bottle looks radioactive, evil. . . . Morphine is a drug

I associate with madness and stupor and tragedy, not with my well-controlled and controlling mother."[30]

The mention of morphine reminds Zoe of hearing the story of twenty-year-old Margaret's visiting her father in a New York hotel room and watching him inject himself with it and her own use of illegal drugs at seventeen. Sent to an "ecology camp" in Nevada, supervised by a counselor nicknamed "Weed," Zoe learns to be a "junkie." Her usage discovered after her return home, she assures her mother, "'It's not that big a deal, Momma. It really didn't affect me that much.' But it wasn't true. I'd loved the dizzy, disconnected feeling it gave me. . . . I knew it was a promise I'd never keep. Taking drugs had inducted me into a secret society, an alternate universe of empty attics and deserted parks, roach clips and wrinkled Baggies."[31]

Margaret's and Zoe's dishonest and distorted thinking about "drugs" becomes a source of their own misery. They reject suicide by Seconal and other drugs and choose death by starvation, which turns out to be protracted, painful, and undignified—a model "imperfect ending":

An overdose is an overdose, and this is exactly the scenario that Hannah, Katherine, and I wanted to avoid. Not only did the idea of watching my mother take pills or morphine repulse me, my sisters and I stood to gain financially [evidently substantial bequests] from her death. What was to stop some overzealous prosecutor from deciding that we had grown tired of waiting for our inheritance? . . . Stopping eating and drinking will allow us to be with her at the end, I say, without legal risk. It's that simple. . . . It suddenly seems imperative to me that she choose that method of death.[32]

Predictably, mother and daughters' mindless efforts fail. Margaret starves and suffers but fails to die. She asks her daughters' permission to take morphine. The day for the final act of the drama finally arrives. Jack joins the sisters. Zoe's fear of being formally blamed for her mother's assisted suicide escalates. Margaret asks how much morphine to take:

> Hannah, who's sitting next to my mother's bed, reaches over and takes the bottle, looks at the label for a moment, and hands it to Jack. Mesmerized, I watch from the couch. . . . I start to shiver. . . . They are talking about milliliters and ounces and droppers. It's a conversation I can't follow. . . . I can see their mouths moving but can barely hear them over the roaring voice inside my head: DON'T TOUCH THAT BOTTLE. Except it's too late, they've touched it. Both of them. And all I can think about is that their fingerprints are on it and that, we're arrested for murder, I'll be the only one able to say I had nothing to do with it, the bottle was never in my hands.[33]

On cue, Margaret reasserts herself: she drops the bottle of morphine, spilling some of its contents. Hannah picks it up, hands it back to her, and waits until she drinks its content: "'I just didn't like handing it to her,' she says angrily. . . . I can tell she is still upset about the dropped bottle. I want to tell her it's okay. That she did what she had to do. And I want to tell her how much I owe her for stepping into the breach tonight, taking on the heaviest burden while I cowered fearfully in the corner.'"[34]

One finishes reading *Imperfect Endings* wondering what made Carter write and publish this pathetic confessional, incriminating both her mother and herself as morally deficient individuals. That she has produced a worthwhile contribution to the literature on assisted suicide? The editors of the *Washington Post* evidently thought so. On March 17, 2010, the paper published a long review-essay, quoting Zoe Carter concluding, "In the end, I thought she [Margaret] had a beautiful and dignified death."[35] Nowhere in her book does Carter assert this patent untruth, inconsistent with its very title. In fact, Carter paints her mother's death, and life, as ugly and undignified, recalling, for example, her wailing, "'I need a parent.' Is that what she wants me to be—her parent? . . . Of course she's afraid. But I am also afraid and I also need a parent."[36] It is no excuse that mother and daughter alike are the products of long-term psychotherapy aimed at validating moral weakness as faultless medical illness.

Although Carter says little directly about suicide prohibition, what she does say is inaccurate and self-serving: "If assisted suicide was legal, and we hadn't been forced to spend so much time worrying about getting caught, we might have been able to better prepare ourselves."[37] Carter and company were not "forced to spend time worrying about getting caught." Gutless, ill-informed, confused, they chose to do so. In fact, Zoe Carter was not really interested in suicide—that is, autohomicide—which she viewed as a job to be delegated to hired help.

Let us here recall Steven Schnipper's suicide, mentioned in chapter 1. What made Schnipper's unassisted suicide so bad that its very nature had to be buried with him? What made Ratcliff's assisted suicide so good that its story is deemed important and uplifting enough to be published by a leading publisher and praised by respectable reviewers? Is it that Schnipper acted alone, exiting life by himself, and Ratcliff did not? Schnipper killed himself, in private, without burdening others with his voluntary exit from life. Ratcliff turned her exit into a family Grand Guignol.

Is this where our "medical ethics"—with its pretended devotion to "benevolence, beneficence, and patient autonomy"—has brought us? To where a daughter is afraid to be present when her mother dies, lest she, the daughter, be charged with murder? Advocates of our suicide prohibition policies might call this an unintended consequence of our meritorious efforts to prevent "drug abuse" and suicide. I contend that it is not, that anyone with a modicum of skepticism about medical ethics and the therapeutic state could have anticipated and predicted precisely such an outcome.

A comparison of these two accounts of voluntary death highlights a disturbing aspect of our contemporary culture, namely, our fear and hatred of autonomy, of self-reliance, of taking care of our business without unnecessarily burdening others with it. We have transformed our old ethic of self-reliance from virtue into vice. We must not be responsible—for our children's education, our medical care, our economic support in old age. As soon as we acquire a measure of self-control, we must begin to relinquish it and acquiesce in being "taken care of" by benevolent agents of the therapeutic state.

5

The Shame of Medicine

1

Throughout most of history, medical care was a personal service provided by physicians to individuals who sought their help. The recipient-patient selected the individual whose assistance he desired and paid for the service he received. By paying for the help, he implicitly consented to the intervention. That relationship is what we mean by a private, personal medical service.

Since ancient times, there has existed another kind of medical service as well, exemplified by Greek slave owners procuring medical assistance for their slaves. In the *Laws*, Plato (428–348 BCE) contrasts the two arrangements as follows:

> Now have you further observed that, as there are slaves as well as free men among the patients of our communities, the slaves, to speak generally, are treated by slaves, who pay them a hurried visit, or receive them in dispensaries? A physician of this kind never gives the servant any account of his complaint, nor asks him for any; he gives him some empirical injunction with an air of finished knowledge, in the brusque fashion of a dictator, and then is off in hot haste to the next ailing servant—that is how he lightens his master's medical labors for him. The free practitioner, who, for the most part, attends free men, treats their diseases by going into things thoroughly from the beginning in a scientific way, and takes the patient and his

family into his confidence. Thus he learns something from the
sufferer, and at the same time instructs the invalid to the best
of his powers. He does not give his prescriptions until he has
won the patient's support, and when he has done so, he steadily
aims at producing complete restoration to health.[1]

Today, in most countries, some people are provided with
medical care by the state as a social service, while others pur-
chase it for themselves from a medical professional as a personal
service. In both systems the payer maintains, or tries to maintain,
control over the parameters of the transaction.

The advent of mad-doctoring conducted in *private madhouses*
in eighteenth-century England introduced a novel element into
the doctor-patient relationship: coercion of the insane, that is,
the use of state-authorized force to provide a "service" de facto
against the patient's will, but de jure for his benefit. Since then,
the practice of psychiatry has rested squarely on coercion. Moreover, unlike a century or two ago when the inherently paternal-
istic-despotic character of mad-doctoring was widely recognized,
today, with psychiatry legally defined as a medical specialty, it is
bad form to notice or mention it. The polite thing is to emphasize
the similarities between (consensual) medical practice and (coercive) psychiatric practice.

I have long maintained that *incarceration in a mental hospital is
unlawful deprivation of liberty, that mental illnesses are fictitious diseases, and that coercive psychiatry is social control, not medical care.*
Viewing involuntary psychiatry as an institution similar to involuntary labor, the aim of my critique was the abolition of psychiatric slavery, not its "reform" and replacement by a "better" system.
Unsurprisingly, this view did not gain professional support. On
the contrary, in the past half century we have witnessed the exten-
sion of coercive psychiatric practices from the closed wards of the
mental hospital into every nook and cranny of the community.

2

For millennia, the medico-ethical principle primum non nocere (first, do no harm)—attributed to Hippocrates—served as an adequate moral guide for the physician's relationship with his patient. This rule works well so long as doctor and patient agree on what counts as harm and what counts as help. It stops working once the parties disagree. It breaks down completely if the doctor defines his proposed intervention as therapy, the patient as torture, and if the doctor has the duty and the power to impose his intervention on the patient against his will. This outcome is what happened when doctors of the mind (psychiatrists) replaced doctors of the soul (clergymen) and were empowered by the state to treat "insane" persons as mentally unfit and decide what is in their wards' best interest. Thenceforth, the principle primum non nocere became the source of an unending series of heartrending tragedies—medical, legal, economic, and social. Henceforth, psychiatrists needed to be restrained by the principle of primum non coercere (first, do not coerce). They were not, and the tragic tale of psychiatry unfolded.

The intention to kill oneself is not an illness, much less is thinking about suicide. Both are fundamental expressions of our existential condition as free and self-conscious individuals. Depriving a person of liberty is not a form of medical treatment. What, then, makes suicide a doctor's business? Why is suicide prevention an integral part of psychiatry? The answers lie in history.

In early Christianity, suicide, not yet of religious concern, was a private affair. By the Middle Ages, self-murder was a grave sin, punishable by eternal damnation in hell. After the Enlightenment and the rise of science, psychiatrists gradually replaced the social functions traditionally performed by clergymen. The medicalization of suicide was part of the creation of psychiatry: suicide as sin became suicide as sickness, and punishment in the hereafter by burning in hell was transformed into punishment in the here and now by incarceration in the insane asylum. The premise that suicide is mental illness and that suicide prevention is psychiatric treatment is so integral to psychiatry as a medical specialty that the very idea of noncoercive psychiatry is an oxymoron.

3

Formerly, inquisitors *tortured* people. Today, by definition, no official holder of power tortures. When spy agencies or military forces use torture, they call it *homeland defense* or *fighting the war on terror*. When mental hospitals and psychiatrists use torture, they call it *suicide prevention*.

Everyone knows that preventing the death of a person intent on killing himself is impossible, except perhaps by the most extraordinary means. At the same time, the more the idea that suicide is caused by mental illness and that its prevention is the duty of the psychiatrist gains popularity, the more convincing becomes the argument that failure to prevent the suicide of the patient—inferred from his successful suicide—is evidence of malpractice. The practical consequences of this mind-set are many and, for the most part, familiar. An unfamiliar aspect of it is the continued demand for more technically sophisticated methods of preventing suicide and a market in extraordinary means of personal restraint.

As one might expect, the market in the incapacitation of persons "dangerous to themselves" developed in tandem with the birth and growth of asylum-hospital psychiatry—hence, the popular association of straitjackets with madhouses. Of course, the decline in old-fashioned mad-housing that began in the 1960s was not accompanied by a decrease in suicides, with the result that the demand for extraordinary methods of personal restraint increased.

If it is not the psychiatrist's business to save the lives of would-be suicides, then whose business is it? The question is moot: the concepts "suicide," "psychiatry," and "coercion" are now inseparable, each implying and entailing the others. If suicide were to be declared a nondisease—a human predilection or act outside the remit of medicine-psychiatry—it would destroy the justification for commitment (sectioning) and, indeed, for all mental health laws. *The psychiatrist's professional identity depends on his being in the lifesaving business, that is, saving the lives of would-be suicides.* Lacking credible competence to treat bodily ailments, the psychiatrist cannot relinquish his role as lifesaver and remain a bona fide medical professional.

In this respect, suicide differs from other nondiseases that psychiatrists have laid claim to—for example, homosexuality. The psychiatrist's medical identity did not depend on persecuting homosexuals; hence, he could relinquish this part of his professional repertoire. The justification of coercive psychiatric suicide prevention is a struggle for the heart and soul—the very existence—of psychiatry. "Many of the most pressing problems of current clinical practice [in psychiatry] turn on questions of risk—balancing care and control in the management of suicide," write Donna Dickenson and Bill (K. W. M.) Fulford, two of the leading contemporary philosophers of psychiatry.[2] These authors do not question the moral legitimacy of psychiatric interference in the lives of so-called suicidal persons, nor do they recognize that their idea of psychiatry rests on the assumption that psychiatry is a bona fide branch of medicine.

To be sure, persons who injure themselves in the process of their failed or faked suicide attempt are *sick*. If they consent to treatment or are unconscious, they are appropriately treated by physicians. If not, they are *not (voluntary) patients*, though, from a biological point of view, they may be sick. If their act is defined as a crime, they ought to be dealt with as lawbreakers. If it is not, they ought to be left alone.

4

The sense that our life is no longer worth living—the "condition" we sometimes call a "mental illness"—is, without doubt, one of the most "painful" of all personal experiences. Such suffering is, however, not per se an illness or medical problem. It is a philosophical and moral problem. Insofar as we communicate our suffering to persons close to us, our suffering becomes a problem for them as well. Any attempt to *forcibly* interfere with the life of such a sufferer converts his private personal problem into a public political one. This point is the vexing issue that underlies the medicalization of suicide and its penumbra—suicidality, suicidal ideation, suicide prevention, coerced psychiatric "care," and related actions and notions.

To think seriously about a phenomenon that common sense as well as science define as a medical-psychiatric problem, we must reconsider some elementary ideas, in this case the nature and purpose of the political community or state. It suffices to note here that, throughout history, people of all kinds have found it useful to come together for the common defense. Against what danger? The wording of a document familiar to most everyone reading these words answers that question succinctly and without equivocation: "I, _____, do solemnly swear (or affirm) that I will support and defend the Constitution of the United States against all enemies, foreign and domestic . . ." So reads the oath of enlistment for individuals joining the armed forces of the United States. There are many dangers facing members of the armed forces, but the oath does not mention any of them. Not every problem is the business of the armed forces, nor is every problem the business of the coercive apparatus of our civilian social control system.

To be sure, the control of certain contagious diseases, usually classified as "public health problems," may require and justify the use of certain coercive measures. But so-called dangerousness to self is not one of them. Nevertheless, in all "progressive" countries, medicine, law, and politics combine to combat the individual's elementary right to voluntarily end his life. This feat is accomplished by means of a special set of laws, neither civil nor criminal, called "mental health laws."

One of the consequences of the medicalization of suicide is the demand for mental health services by the parents of children who threaten to kill themselves. Suicide as blackmail in the family thus turns into suicide as blackmail in society at large. A report, titled "Families Worry Mental Health Cuts Will Send Kids Spiraling: Services for 20,000 California Students May Be in Jeopardy Because of a Schwarzenegger Veto of Funding; A Class-Action Suit Seeks to Keep the Services as They Are," in the *Los Angeles Times* in December 2010, describes the process:

A week before Christmas, Judy Powelson was awaiting her son's first visit home in nine months with a mix of excitement and trepidation. Earlier in the year, the 17-year-old's mental illness had spiraled out of control to the point that he attacked her, kicked a teacher in the groin and was hospitalized for psychiatric treatment. But since he entered residential treatment funded in part by the state, she'd seen him go through marked improvements. . . . Now Powelson's son, identified in court papers as T.G., is one of 20,000 students across California whose mental health services may be in jeopardy in the new year because of a line-item veto by the governor. . . . Families with children who suffer from mental illnesses ranging from depression to schizophrenia and who depend on these services have been thrown into chaos, parents and advocates say. . . ."If my son loses this treatment, I will lose my son," Powelson said, her voice quivering. "I will lose him to mental illness, I will lose him to the criminal justice system, to drug abuse, to *suicide*." . . . David Campos, whose son is the lead plaintiff, said he felt his child was being left behind while government agencies passed the blame. . . . Campos and his wife, Gail, have been trying to get help for their son ever since they adopted him at age 4, knowing he suffered the effects of fetal alcohol syndrome and had been neglected and abused. This summer, their son twice attempted *suicide*—swallowing half a bottle of Tylenol and trying to hang himself—and landed in juvenile hall.[3]

Although modern psychiatrists pretend that coerced-involuntary psychiatric confinement ("hospitalization") and psychiatric torture ("treatment") are relics of long-past psychiatric abuses, the truth is that the psychiatric community as well as the popular press unceasingly agitate for ever more psychiatric coercions, not only for persons incarcerated in mental hospitals but also for persons living in their own homes.

This confinement is euphemistically called Assertive Community Treatment (ACT) or Outpatient Commitment. In effect, it is a kind of psychiatric parole, judges ordering persons whom psychiatrists declare to be suffering from mental illnesses and to be refusing treatment to comply with their physicians' orders to ingest the psychiatric drugs they have prescribed for them or else be committed to an insane asylum and there be forcibly medicated.

E. Fuller Torrey is probably the best-known American advocate of ACT. Writing in May 2010 in the *New York Times*, he laments that some critics of the practice oppose "psychiatric treatment by court order, supposedly violating the patients' freedom to choose or forgo treatment. But these are people whose illness interferes with their ability to understand that they are sick and need medication." Citing the case of the perpetrator of a much-publicized crime, whose act Torrey attributes to "taking orders from his psychotic brain," Torrey concludes that such persons "do not have the choice to live freely and comfortably, but only to be homeless, in jail or in a psychiatric hospital."[4]

Psychiatric dramatizations, enlivened by base rhetoric—such as the phrase "taking orders from psychotic brains"—confuse the public by conflating autohomicide and heterohomicide, killing oneself and killing another. Pretending to be the pride of medicine, psychiatry is its shame.

6

Envoi

IN "THE MYTH OF SISYPHUS" (1942), Albert Camus famously declares, "There is but one truly serious philosophical problem, and that is suicide."[1] Seventy years later, everyone knows that suicide is a psychiatric emergency, not a philosophical problem.

Ostensibly, contemporary discourse about suicide concerns understanding the individual who says he intends to kill himself or, perhaps more often, the individual to whom such intention is attributed by others. In fact, its true subject is the imperiled professional identity of the psychiatrist as bona fide physician, contingent on his presumed medical competence and legal duty to "save lives," especially the lives of persons who do not want to live.

Understanding a person and coercing him are mutually antagonistic and incompatible functions and roles, and we all know it. I have long objected to the social expectation that the psychiatrist be both consensual healer of souls *and* coercive controller of misbehaving persons and to the psychiatrist's willingness to play both roles. The moral dilemma of double agency is built into psychiatry and will not go away. Honest psychiatrists cannot help but confront it. Hapless patients are doomed to be injured by it.

That medicalization forms an integral part of the modern zeitgeist is obvious. Some fifty years ago I coined the term *therapeutic state* and suggested that coercive psychiatric suicide prevention is one of its defining emblems. Opposing this revered ritual may be a thankless task, but is a worthy goal.

"The time is out of joint—O cursed spite, / That ever I was born to set it right!" soliloquizes Hamlet (1.5.188–90). For the lover of liberty and responsibility, the time always seems out of joint. The individual who assumes the task of setting such dislocations aright runs the risk of being destroyed in the process. I bless my stars for protecting me from that fate, and thank my family, friends, and colleagues for helping me protect myself from it.

APPENDIX

NOTES

BIBLIOGRAPHY

INDEX

APPENDIX: *"On Suicide" by David Hume*

The "principle of self-ownership"—one of the bedrock premises of modern libertarianism—was fully articulated by the Scottish philosopher David Hume. His essay "On Suicide" is a pioneering defense of our "right" to end our own lives. Composed probably in 1755, published posthumously in 1777, "On Suicide" runs to a mere eleven pages. I have selected the passages most pertinent to the contemporary debate:

> The lives of men depend upon the same laws as the lives of all other animals; and these are subjected to the general laws of matter and motion. . . . Since therefore the lives of men are for ever dependant on the general laws of matter and motion, is a man's disposing of his life criminal, because in every case it is criminal to encroach upon these laws, or disturb their operation? But this seems absurd; all animals are entrusted to their own prudence and skill for their conduct in the world, and have full authority as far as their power extends, to alter all the operations of nature. Without the exercise of this authority they could not subsist a moment; every action, every motion of a man, innovates on the order of some parts of matter, and diverts from their ordinary course the general laws of motion. Putting together, therefore, these conclusions, we find that human life depends upon the general laws of matter and motion, and that it is no encroachment on the office of providence to disturb or alter these general laws: Has not every one, of consequence, the free disposal of his own life? And may he not lawfully employ that power with which nature has endowed him? In order to

destroy the evidence of this conclusion, we must shew a reason why this particular case is excepted; is it because human life is of such great importance, that 'tis a presumption for human prudence to dispose of it? But the life of a man is of no greater importance to the universe than that of an oyster. . . . Were the disposal of human life so much reserved as the peculiar province of the Almighty, that it were an encroachment on his right, for men to dispose of their own lives; it would be equally criminal to act for the preservation of life as for its destruction. If I turn aside a stone which is falling upon my head, I disturb the course of nature, and I invade the peculiar province of the Almighty, by lengthening out my life beyond the period which by the general laws of matter and motion he had assigned it. A hair, a fly, an insect is able to destroy this mighty being whose life is of such importance. . . . To you it belongs to repine at providence, who foolishly imagine that you have no such power, and who must still prolong a hated life, tho' loaded with pain and sickness, with shame and poverty. Do not you teach, that when any ill befalls me, tho' by the malice of my enemies, I ought to be resigned to providence, and that the actions of men are the operations of the Almighty as much as the actions of inanimate beings? When I fall upon my own sword, therefore, I receive my death equally from the hands of the Deity as if it had proceeded from a lion, a precipice, or a fever. The submission which you require to providence, in every calamity that befalls me, excludes not human skill and industry, if possible by their means I can avoid or escape the calamity: And why may I not employ one remedy as well as another? If my life be not my own, it were criminal for me to put it in danger, as well as to dispose of it. . . . There is no being, which possesses any power or faculty, that it receives not from its Creator, nor is there any one, which by ever so irregular an action can encroach upon the plan of his providence, or disorder the universe. Its operations are his works equally with that chain of events which it invades, and which ever principle prevails, we may for that very reason conclude it to be most favoured by him. Be it animate, or inanimate, rational, or irrational, 'tis all a case: its power is still derived from the supreme Creator, and is alike comprehended in the order of his providence. When the horror of pain prevails over the love of life; when a voluntary action anticipates the effects of blind causes, 'tis only in consequence of those powers and principles which he has implanted in his creatures. Divine providence is still inviolate, and placed far beyond the reach of human injuries. 'Tis impious says the old Roman superstition to divert rivers from their course, or invade the prerogatives of nature. 'Tis impious says the French superstition to inoculate for the small-pox, or usurp the business of providence by voluntarily producing distempers and maladies. 'Tis impious says the modern European superstition, to put a period to our own life, and thereby rebel against our Creator; and why not impious, say I, to build houses, cultivate the ground, or sail upon the ocean? In all these actions we employ our powers of mind and body, to produce some innovation in the course of nature; and in none of them do we any more. They are all of them therefore equally innocent, or equally criminal.[1]

Notes

Preface

1. R. Daly, "End Ban on Condolences After Soldier Dies by Suicide, APA Says," *Psychiatric News* 45 (Nov. 19, 2010): 2, http://pn.psychiatryonline.org/content/45/22/2.4.full.

2. http://www.historyofpia.com/forums/viewtopic.php?f=3&t=12515&start =0.

3. J. W. von Goethe, *The Truth and Fiction Relating to My Life*, in *The Complete Works of Johann Wolfgang von Goethe*, trans. J. Oxenford, 10 vols. (New York: P. F. Collier and Son, n.d.), 2:163.

4. D. Hume, "On Suicide" (1777), in *Essays: Moral, Political, and Literary*, D. Hume, ed. Eugene F. Miller, rev. ed. (Indianapolis: Liberty Fund, 1985), 577–89. See also the appendix.

5. B. Rush, "The Founders' Constitution," vol. 5, amendment 8, doc. 16, in *The Selected Writings of Benjamin Rush*, ed. D. D. Runes (New York: Philosophical Library, 1947), http://press-pubs.uchicago.edu/founders/documents/amendVIIIs16.html; *Lectures on the Medical Jurisprudence of the Mind* (1810), in *The Autobiography of Benjamin Rush: His "Travels Through Life" Together with His "Commonplace Book for 1789–1812,"* ed. G. W. Corner (Princeton: Princeton Univ. Press, 1948), 350; *Medical Inquiries and Observations upon the Diseases of the Mind* (1812) (New York: Hafner Press, 1962), 273–74.

6. "What Is It Like to Be Committed to the Psychiatric Ward of a Hospital?" (2001), http://www.antipsychiatry.org/e-mail.htm.

7. In this book I use many common terms—such as *mental illness, psychiatric treatment, suicide prevention,* and others—with the understanding that I do not share their conventional meanings or connotations.

8. My opposition to medical coercions is limited to adults. Children are not legally qualified to consent to receive, or reject, medical services.

Introduction

1. T. Szasz, *Fatal Freedom: The Ethics and Politics of Suicide*, esp. 129–31. The term *death control* now appears on some Web sites: for example, J. R. Mooneyham, "The Second Coming: What Will Happen to the World Once a Practical Death Control Pill Becomes Widely Available?" (2000), http://www.jrmooneyham.com/2com.html.

2. Quoted in H. Arendt, *Eichmann in Jerusalem: A Report on the Banality of Evil*, 64.

3. T. Szasz, *Pharmacracy: Medicine and Politics in America*.

4. http://en.wikipedia.org/wiki/List_of_countries_by_suicide_rate.

5. "Federal Commitment to Suicide Prevention: A Call to Collaboration," http://www.sprc.org/library/collabcall.pdf (emphasis added).

6. Ibid. (emphasis added).

7. Ibid. (emphasis added).

8. G. Wilkinson, "Can Suicide Be Prevented?" *British Medical Journal* 309 (Oct. 1994): 860–62.

9. T. Szasz, *The Myth of Psychotherapy: Mental Healing as Religion, Rhetoric, and Repression*, esp. 67–81.

10. Szasz, *Fatal Freedom*.

11. "Ideation," http://en.wikipedia.org/wiki/Ideation.

12. Szasz, *Pharmacracy*.

13. W. F. Bynum and M. Neve, "Hamlet on the Couch," in *The Anatomy of Madness: Essays in the History of Psychiatry*, vol. 1, *People and Ideas*, ed. W. F. Bynum, R. Porter, and M. Shepherd, 295.

14. Szasz, *Fatal Freedom*, chap. 3.

15. J. S. Mill, *On Liberty* (1859) (Chicago: Regnery, 1955), 14.

16. See T. Szasz, *Coercion as Cure: A Critical History of Psychiatry, Cruel Compassion: The Psychiatric Control of Society's Unwanted, Liberation by Oppression: A Comparative Study of Slavery and Psychiatry*, and *Psychiatry: The Science of Lies*.

17. See T. Szasz, "The Case Against Suicide Prevention," *American Psychologist* 41 (July 1986): 806–12; "Noncoercive Psychiatry: An Oxymoron," *Journal of Humanistic Psychology* 31 (Spring 1991): 117–25; and *Fatal Freedom*.

1. Suicide Prohibition

1. Department of Health and Human Services, CDC (Centers for Disease Control and Prevention), "Youth Suicide." http://www.cdc.gov/ncipc/dvp/suicide/youthsuicide.htm; A. Camus, "The Myth of Sisyphus," 3.

2. M. McDonald and T. R. Murphy, *Sleepless Souls: Suicide in Early Modern England*. See also Szasz, *Fatal Freedom*.

3. The psychiatric detention of Alice Battenberg (Mountbatten)—the mother of Philip Mountbatten, husband of Queen Elizabeth II of Great Britain—is a dramatic example. H. Vickers, *Alice: Princess Andrew of Greece*.

4. W. H. Auden, "In Memoriam of Sigmund Freud" (1940), http://www.poets.org/viewmedia.php/prmMID/15543.

5. S. K. Schwartz, "Is It Ever OK to Lie to Patients?" *Physicians Practice* 20 (Nov. 2010): 43–45, http://www.physicianspractice.com/difficult-patients/content/article/1462168/1700578.

6. Szasz, *Psychiatry: The Science of Lies*.

7. M. Goin, "The 'Suicide-Prevention Contract': A Dangerous Myth," *Psychiatric News* 38 (July 18, 2003): 3, 27, http://pn.psychiatryonline.org/cgi/content/full/38/14/3.

8. F. K. Wong, A. Wolanin, and P. Smallwood, "The Suicidal Patient," in *Clinical Manual of Emergency Psychiatry*, ed. M. B. Riba and D. Ravindranath, 53–54.

9. H. S. Maine, *Ancient Law: Its Connection with the Early History of Society, and Its Relation to Modern Ideas* (1864; reprint, Tucson: Univ. of Arizona Press, 1986), 163–65 (emphasis added).

10. "The Star-Spangled Banner," http://en.wikipedia.org/wiki/The_Star-Spangled_Banner.

11. http://en.wikipedia.org/wiki/Article_One_of_the_United_States_Constitution.

12. R. E. DeMartino et al., "A Call to Collaboration: Federal Commitment to Suicide Prevention" (2003), http://www.sprc.org/library/collabcall.pdf.

13. T. Szasz, "The Socrates Option," *Reason* 24 (Apr. 1992): 47.

14. T. Gabriel, "After 3 Suspected Suicides, Cornell Reaches Out," *New York Times*, Mar. 16, 2010, http://www.nytimes.com/2010/03/17/education/17cornell.html?scp=1&sq=after%20three%20suspected%.

15. D. J. Skorton, "Cornell's President, on Suicide Among the Young" (Letters), *New York Times*, Mar. 23, 2010, http://www.nytimes.com/2010/03/24/opinion/l24cornell.html?ref=todayspaper.

16. T. Szasz, "College Psychiatry: A Critique," *Comprehensive Psychiatry* 9 (Jan. 1968): 81–85.

17. J. Johnson, "Third Suicide This Year at William & Mary Highlights Challenges of Prevention," *Washington Post*, Nov. 13, 2010, http://www.washingtonpost.com/wp-dyn/content/article/2010/11/12/AR2010111202853.html. Subsequent quotes are from this source.

18. In re R.F., Appeal of R.F., Superior Court of Pennsylvania, Submitted Sept. 11, 2006, Filed Dec. 27, 2006.

19. Superior Court of Pennsylvania, In re S.B., Appeal of S.B., Argued Sept. 12, 2000, Filed Dec. 1, 2000. I thank Professor Alexander Tsesis for providing me with these records.

20. See A. Margalit, *The Decent Society* (Cambridge: Harvard Univ. Press, 1996) and *The Ethics of Memory* (Cambridge: Harvard Univ. Press, 2002).

21. T. Szasz, "Whither Psychiatry?" *Social Research* 33 (Autumn 1966): 439–62.

22. Quoted in J. Todd, *Mary Wollstonecraft: A Revolutionary Life*, 484.

23. Ibid., 356.

24. Ibid.

25. Royal Humane Society, http://www.royalhumanesociety.org.uk/.

26. American Foundation for Suicide Prevention, http://www.afsp.org/.

27. Szasz, *Fatal Freedom*.

28. M. Winerip, "A Life on the Decline, and Then the 'Why?'" *New York Times*, Sept. 18, 2009, http://www.nytimes.com/2009/09/20/fashion/20genb.html?page wanted=.

29. G. Paton, "Chris Woodhead 'Considering Suicide' After Motor Neurone Disease Diagnosis," *Telegraph*, May 9, 2009, http://www.telegraph.co.uk/education/educationnews/5267559/Chris-Woodhead-considering-suicide-after-motor-neurone-disease-diagnosis.html.

30. T. Hobson, "We Must Keep the Taboo Against Suicide," *Guardian*, May 6, 2009, http://www.guardian.co.uk/commentisfree/belief/2009/may/06/suicide-motor-neurone-woodhead (emphasis added).

31. Quoted in D. J. Boorstin, *The Lost World of Thomas Jefferson* (Boston: Beacon Press, 1948), 182; and in L. H. Butterfield, ed., *Letters of Benjamin Rush* (Princeton: Princeton Univ. Press, 1951), 1092.

32. Rush, *Lectures on the Medical Jurisprudence of the Mind*, 350 (see preface, n. 5). For more about Rush, see T. Szasz, *The Manufacture of Madness: A Comparative Study of the Inquisition and the Mental Health Movement* and *Coercion as Cure*.

33. M. Bowker, "Opposition Flows from a Fear of Accepting Care," *Buffalo News*, Mar. 30, 2010, http://www.buffalonews.com/2010/03/24/997411/opposition-flows-from-a-fear-of.html.

34. "The Law of Momentum Conservation," http://www.physicsclassroom.com/class/momentum/u4l2a.cfm.

35. "Church of Euthanasia," http://en.wikipedia.org/wiki/Church_of_Euthanasia.

2. The Suicide Prohibition Agent

1. T. Szasz, *Our Right to Drugs: The Case for a Free Market.*

2. J. Holland, *Weekends at Bellevue* (New York: Bantam Books, 2009), 13.

3. Ibid., 254–55.

4. P. R. Linde, *Danger to Self: On the Front Line with an ER Psychiatrist,* xiii.

5. "Emergency Psychiatry," http://en.wikipedia.org/wiki/Emergency_psychiatry.

6. Ibid., 1. The reference is to R. D. Laing, *Wisdom, Madness, and Folly: The Making of a Psychiatrist,* 55. Linde then proceeds to link my name with Laing's, as if our views were interchangeable.

7. E. Bleuler, *Dementia Praecox; or, The Group of Schizophrenias,* trans. J. Zinkin (1911; reprint, New York: International Universities Press, 1950), 488–89.

8. D. Elkin, P. R. Linde, and E. Woodward, "A Day in the Life of PES: Twenty-four Hours at the Psychiatric Emergency Services Department of San Francisco General Hospital," *San Francisco Medicine* 82, no. 2 (2009), http://www.paullinde.com/.

9. Ibid.

10. Linde, *Danger to Self,* 102.

11. Ibid.

12. "5150 (Involuntary Psychiatric Hold)," http://en.wikipedia.org/wiki/5150_(Involuntary_psychiatric_hold).

13. Elkin, Linde, and Woodward, "A Day in the Life of PES."

14. Linde, *Danger to Self,* 100.

15. *Donaldson v. O'Connor,* 493 F.2d 507 (1974). See also T. Szasz, *Psychiatric Slavery: When Confinement and Coercion Masquerade as Cure,* reprinted with a new preface as *Psychiatric Slavery.*

16. Quoted in Szasz, *Psychiatric Slavery,* 20.

17. K. Donaldson, *Insanity Inside Out* (New York: Crown, 1976) and "Blazing a Trail for Mental Patients Who Want to Get Out: Kenneth Donaldson Tells His Own Story," *Harper's Weekly,* July 25, 1975.

18. Quoted in Szasz, *Psychiatric Slavery,* 21ff.

19. Ibid., 25, 26–27.

20. See Szasz, *Liberation by Oppression.*

21. Linde, *Danger to Self,* 100.

22. Ibid., 101–2.

23. Ibid., 117–18.

24. Ibid., 118.

25. T. Szasz, *Insanity: The Idea and Its Consequences*, 91. See also "Liberty and the Practice of Psychotherapy: Interview with Randall C. Wyatt," *Journal of Humanistic Psychology* 44 (Jan. 2004): 71–85, http://jhp.sagepub.com/content/44/1/71.short.

26. Linde, *Danger to Self*, 137.

27. J. Johnson, "U-Va. to Scrutinize *Virginia Quarterly Review* After Editor's Suicide," *Washington Post*, Aug. 20, 2010, http://www.washingtonpost.com/wp-dyn/content/article/2010/08/19/AR2010081906493.html; J. Bosman, "Esteemed Literary Journal Closes Offices After Suicide," *New York Times*, Aug. 30, 2010, http://artsbeat.blogs.nytimes.com/2010/08/30/esteemed-literary-journal-closes-offices-after-suicide/?hp.

28. T. E. Pytell, "Redeeming the Unredeemable: Auschwitz and Man's Search for Meaning," *Holocaust and Genocide Studies* 17 (2003): 89–113.

29. V. E. Frankl, *Man's Search for Meaning*, 134.

30. "Viktor Frankl," http://en.wikipedia.org/wiki/Viktor_Frankl.

31. Pytell, "Redeeming the Unredeemable."

32. Frankl, *Man's Search for Meaning*, 25 (emphasis added); V. E. Frankl, "'Nothing but': On Reductionism and Nihilism," *Encounter* (London) 33 (Nov. 1969): 55 (emphasis added).

33. Pytell, "Redeeming the Unredeemable."

34. Ibid.

35. Frankl, *Man's Search for Meaning*, 86, 36ff.

36. Szasz, *Fatal Freedom*, 89–105.

37. http://www.reference.com/browse/wiki/Viktor_Frankl.

38. L. L. Langer, *Versions of Survival: The Holocaust and the Human Spirit*, 24; Frankl, *Man's Search for Meaning*, 66–67.

39. V. E. Frankl quoted in M. Scully, "Viktor Frankl at Ninety: An Interview," *First Things* 52 (Apr. 1995): 39–43, http://www.leaderu.com/ftissues/ft9504/articles/scully.html.

40. Langer, *Versions of Survival*, 22–24; Pytell, "Redeeming the Unredeemable."

41. Ibid.

42. Langer, *Versions of Survival*, 95.

43. Pytell, "Redeeming the Unredeemable." *Arbeit Macht Frei* (Work will make you free) was the slogan over the entrance to Auschwitz.

44. D. G. Myers, "Jean Améry: A Biographical Introduction," in *Holocaust Literature: An Encyclopedia of Writers and Their Work*, ed. S. L. Kremer (New York: Routledge, 2002), http://www-english.tamu.edu/pers/fac/myers/amery.html. Subsequent quotations are from this source unless otherwise indicated.

45. J. Améry, *At the Mind's Limits: Contemplations by a Survivor on Auschwitz and Its Realities*, 97.

46. J. Améry, *On Suicide: A Discourse on Voluntary Death*, 16.

47. Ibid., 93–94.

48. Ibid., 52.

49. R. Bayer, *Homosexuality and American Psychiatry: The Politics of Diagnosis*, 11.

3. The Marriage of Asclepius and Atropos

1. R. E. DeMartino et al., "A Call to Collaboration: Federal Commitment to Suicide Prevention" (2003), http://www.sprc.org/library/collabcall.pdf.

2. Szasz, *Coercion as Cure*.

3. A. Deutsch, *The Shame of the States*.

4. A. Deutsch, *The Mentally Ill in America: A History of Their Care and Treatment from Colonial Times*, 153, 151.

5. Ibid., 137.

6. D. Dix, quoted in ibid., 177.

7. "Franklin Pierce's Veto of May 3, 1854," http://www.disabilitymuseum .org/ib/docs/682.htm (emphasis added).

8. Szasz, *Cruel Compassion*, 158–79.

9. J. F. Kennedy, "Message from the President of the United States Relative to Mental Illness and Mental Retardation," Feb. 5, 1963, 88th Cong., 1st sess., H. Rep. Document No. 58.

10. Quoted in Office of the Press Secretary of the President of the United States, "Remarks by the President, the First Lady, the Vice President, and Mrs. Gore at White House Conference on Mental Health," Blackburn Auditorium, Howard Univ., Washington, DC, June 7, 1999, Arianna Online, 1158 26th Street, Suite #428, Santa Monica, CA 90403, E-mail: info@ariannaonline.com, Copyright © 1998 Christabella, Inc.

4. Separation: Emigration, Secession, Suicide

1. K. R. Jamison, *Night Falls Fast: Understanding Suicide*; T. Joiner, *Why People Die by Suicide* (Cambridge: Harvard Univ. Press, 2007).

2. P. Kix, "The Truth About Suicide Bombers: Are They Religious Fanatics? Deluded Ideologues? New Research Suggests Something More Mundane: They Just Want to Commit Suicide," *Boston Globe*, Dec. 5, 2010, http://www

.boston.com/bostonglobe/ideas/articles/2010/12/05/the_truth_about_suicide
_bombers/?page=full.

3. National Institute of Mental Health, "Suicide in the U.S.: Statistics and Prevention," http://www.nimh.nih.gov/health/publications/suicide-in-the-us-statistics-and-prevention/index.shtml.

4. Améry, *On Suicide,* 1–2.

5. Szasz, *Fatal Freedom.*

6. Ibid.

7. T. J. DiLorenzo, "Happy Secession Day—July 4, 2006," http://www.lewrockwell.com/dilorenzo/dilorenzo103.html.

8. T. Jefferson, "Letter to William H. Crawford, 1816," in "Articles of Confederation," http://en.wikipedia.org/wiki/Articles_of_Confederation.

9. A. Lincoln, "Letter to Horace Greely, August 22, 1862," in "Abraham Lincoln on Slavery," http://en.wikipedia.org/wiki/Abraham_Lincoln_on_slavery.

10. T. Jefferson, "The Memoir" (1821), in *Memoir, Correspondence, and Miscellanies, from the Papers of Thomas Jefferson,* ed. T. J. Randolph, 6 vols. (New York: Gray and Bowen, 1830), 1:125.

11. T. Jefferson, "Letter to Dr. Samuel Brown," July 14, 1813, in *The Life and Writings of Thomas Jefferson,* ed. A. Koch and W. Peden (New York: Modern Library, 1944), 629.

12. M. Moran, "Psychiatrists Urged to Work with Journalists on Reporting of Suicides," *Psychiatric News* 44 (Apr. 3, 2009): 12, http://pn.psychiatryonline.org/cgi/content/full/44/7/12-a.

13. "Alt.suicide.holiday," http://en.wikipedia.org/wiki/Alt.suicide.holiday.

14. "Usenet," http://en.wikipedia.org/wiki/Usenet.

15. Final Exit Network, http://www.finalexitnetwork.org/ (emphasis added).

16. "Eudaimonia," http://en.wikipedia.org/wiki/Eudaimonia.

17. Z. F. Carter, *Imperfect Endings: A Daughter's Tale of Life and Death* (New York: Simon and Schuster, 2010).

18. See M. Hesse, "Imperfect Endings," *Washington Post,* March 17, 2010, http://www.washingtonpost.com/wp-dyn/content/article/2010/03/16/AR2010031603986.html?wpisrc=nl_pmheadline.

19. Carter, *Imperfect Endings,* 5.

20. Ibid., 24.

21. Ibid., 10–13.

22. Ibid., 35.

23. Ibid., 38–39.

24. Ibid., 23.

25. Ibid., 40, 50.

26. Ibid., 70–71, 146–47.

27. Ibid., 96.

28. Ibid., 97.

29. Ibid., 103.

30. Ibid., 104–5, 108.

31. Ibid., 106–7.

32. Ibid., 115, 117, 118.

33. Ibid., 216.

34. Ibid., 222–23.

35. Quoted in Hesse, "Imperfect Endings."

36. Carter, *Imperfect Endings*, 219.

37. Ibid., 230.

5. The Shame of Medicine

1. Plato, *Laws*, trans. A. E. Taylor, in *The Collected Dialogues of Plato, Including the Letters*, 1310–11.

2. Szasz, *Liberation by Oppression*.

3. V. Kim, "Families Worry Mental Health Cuts Will Send Kids Spiraling: Services for 20,000 California Students May Be in Jeopardy Because of a Schwarzenegger Veto of Funding; A Class-Action Suit Seeks to Keep the Services as They Are," *Los Angeles Times*, Dec. 28, 2010, http://www.latimes.com/health/la-me-mental-health-20101224,0,3330710.story (emphasis added).

4. E. F. Torrey, "Make Kendra's Law Permanent," *New York Times*, May 28, 2010, http://www.nytimes.com/2010/06/01/opinion/01torrey.html?scp=1&sq=torrey&st=cse.

6. Envoi

1. Camus, "The Myth of Sisyphus," 3.

Appendix: "On Suicide" by David Hume

1. Hume, "On Suicide," 577–89 (see preface, n. 4).

Bibliography

Alvarez, A. *The Savage God: A Study of Suicide.* New York: Random House, 1972.

Améry, J. *At the Mind's Limits: Contemplations by a Survivor on Auschwitz and Its Realities.* Trans. S. Rosenfeld and S. P. Rosenfeld. 1966. Reprint, New York: Schocken Books, 1980.

———. *On Suicide: A Discourse on Voluntary Death.* Trans. J. D. Barlow. 1976. Reprint, Bloomington: Indiana Univ. Press, 1999.

Arendt, H. *Eichmann in Jerusalem: A Report on the Banality of Evil.* New York: Viking, 1963.

Auster, P. *The Invention of Solitude: A Memoir.* 1982. Reprint, New York: Penguin, 1988.

Batthyany, A., and J. Levinson, eds. *Existential Psychotherapy of Meaning: A Handbook of Logotherapy and Existential Analysis.* Phoenix: Zeig, Tucker, and Theisen, 2009.

Bayer, R. *Homosexuality and American Psychiatry: The Politics of Diagnosis.* New York: Basic Books, 1981.

Brudholm, T. *Resentment's Virtue: Jean Améry and the Refusal to Forgive.* Philadelphia: Temple Univ. Press, 2008.

Bynum, W. F., R. Porter, and M. Shepherd, eds. *The Anatomy of Madness: Essays in the History of Psychiatry.* Vol. 1, *People and Ideas.* London: Tavistock, 1985.

———. *The Anatomy of Madness: Essays in the History of Psychiatry.* Vol. 2, *Institutions and Society.* London: Tavistock, 1985.

Camus, A. "The Myth of Sisyphus." In *The Myth of Sisyphus, and Other Essays.* Trans. J. O'Brien. 1942. Reprint, New York: Alfred A. Knopf, 1955.

————. *Resistance, Rebellion, and Death.* Trans. J. O'Brien. New York: Alfred A. Knopf, 1961.

Carter, Z. F. *Imperfect Endings: A Daughter's Tale of Life and Death.* New York: Simon and Schuster, 2010.

Cassel. *The New Cassel's German Dictionary.* New York: Funk and Wagnall's, 1958.

Clare, A. *Dissent in Psychiatry: Controversial Issues in Thought and Practice.* London: Tavistock, 1976.

Deutsch, A. *The Mentally Ill in America: A History of Their Care and Treatment from Colonial Times.* 2nd ed. New York: Columbia Univ. Press, 1952.

————. *The Shame of the States.* New York: Harcourt, Brace, 1948.

Dickenson, D., and B. [K. W. M.] Fulford. *In Two Minds: A Casebook of Psychiatric Ethics.* London: Oxford Univ. Press, 2000.

Fairbairn, G. J. *Contemplating Suicide: The Language and Ethics of Suicide.* London: Routledge, 1995.

Frankl, V. E. *The Doctor and the Soul: From Psychotherapy to Logotherapy.* Trans. R. Winston and C. Winston. New York: Alfred A. Knopf, 1955.

————. *Man's Search for Meaning.* 1946. Reprint, Boston: Beacon Press, 2006.

————. *Recollections: An Autobiography.* Trans. J. Fabry and J. Fabry. 1995. Reprint, New York: Plenum Press, 1997.

Glover, J. *Causing Death and Saving Lives.* 1977. Reprint, Harmondsworth, UK: Penguin, 1984.

Goeschel, C. *Suicide in Nazi Germany.* Oxford: Oxford Univ. Press, 2009.

Hayek, F. A. *The Constitution of Liberty.* Chicago: Univ. of Chicago Press, 1960.

Heidelberger-Leonard, I. *The Philosopher of Auschwitz: Jean Améry and Living with the Holocaust.* London: I. B. Tauris, 2010.

Hume, D. *Essays: Moral, Political, and Literary.* Ed. E. F. Miller. Rev. ed. Indianapolis: Liberty Fund, 1985.

Jamison, K. R. *Night Falls Fast: Understanding Suicide.* New York: Alfred A. Knopf, 1999.

————. *An Unquiet Mind: A Memoir of Mood and Madness.* New York: Alfred A. Knopf, 1995.

Kaplan, K. J., and M. B. Schwartz. *A Psychology of Hope: A Biblical Response to Tragedy and Suicide*. Rev. ed. 1993. Reprint, Grand Rapids, MI: William B. Eerdmans, 2008.

Kaplan, M. A. *Between Dignity and Despair: Jewish Life in Nazi Germany*. New York: Oxford Univ. Press, 1998.

Kremer, S. L., ed. *Holocaust Literature: An Encyclopedia of Writers and Their Work*. New York: Routledge, 2002.

Laing, R. D. *Wisdom, Madness, and Folly: The Making of a Psychiatrist*. New York: McGraw-Hill, 1985.

Langer, L. L. *Holocaust Testimonials: The Ruins of Memory*. New Haven: Yale Univ. Press, 1991.

———. *Versions of Survival: The Holocaust and the Human Spirit*. Albany: State Univ. of New York Press, 1982.

Langley, E. *Narcissism and Suicide in Shakespeare and His Contemporaries*. London: Oxford Univ. Press, 2009.

Lester, D. *Fixin' to Die: A Compassionate Guide to Committing Suicide or Staying Alive*. Amityville, NY: Baywood, 2003.

———. *Suicide and the Holocaust*. New York: Nova Science Publishers, 2005.

Levi, P. *The Drowned and the Saved*. New York: Vintage, 1988.

Linde, P. R. *Danger to Self: On the Front Line with an ER Psychiatrist*. Berkeley and Los Angeles: Univ. of California Press, 2010.

Maguire, D. C. *Death by Choice*. New York: Schocken Books, 1975.

McDonald, M., and T. R. Murphy. *Sleepless Souls: Suicide in Early Modern England*. Oxford: Clarendon Press, 1990.

Minois, G. *History of Suicide: Voluntary Death in Western Culture*. Trans. L. G. Cochrane. 1995. Reprint, Baltimore: Johns Hopkins Univ. Press, 1999.

Mises, L. *Human Action: A Treatise on Economics*. New Haven: Yale Univ. Press, 1949.

Murphy, J. G. *Getting Even: Forgiveness and Its Limits*. New York: Oxford Univ. Press, 2004.

Palmer, T. G. *Realizing Freedom: Libertarian Theory, History, and Practice*. Washington, DC: Cato Institute, 2009.

Palyi, M. *Compulsory Medical Care and the Welfare State*. Chicago: National Institute of Professional Services, 1949.

126   •   Bibliography

Plato. *The Collected Dialogues of Plato, Including the Letters.* Ed. E. Hamilton and H. Cairns. Princeton: Princeton Univ. Press, 1961.

Rahe, P. A. *Soft Despotism, Democracy's Drift: Montesquieu, Rousseau, Tocqueville, and the Modern Prospect.* New Haven: Yale Univ. Press, 2009.

Riba, M. B., and D. Ravindranath, eds. *Clinical Manual of Emergency Psychiatry.* Washington, DC: American Psychiatric Publishing, 2010.

Rothbard, M. *For a New Liberty: The Libertarian Manifesto.* Rev. ed. 1973. Reprint, New York: Collier, 1978.

Staël-Holstein, A. L. G. *Reflections on Suicide.* 1813. Reprint, New York: AMS Press, 1975.

Szasz, T., ed. *The Age of Madness: A History of Involuntary Mental Hospitalization Presented in Selected Texts.* Garden City, NY: Doubleday Anchor, 1973.

———. *Coercion as Cure: A Critical History of Psychiatry.* New Brunswick, NJ: Transaction, 2007.

———. *Cruel Compassion: The Psychiatric Control of Society's Unwanted.* 1994. Reprint, Syracuse: Syracuse Univ. Press, 1998.

———. *The Ethics of Psychoanalysis: The Theory and Method of Autonomous Psychotherapy.* 1965. Syracuse: Syracuse Univ. Press, 1988.

———. *Faith in Freedom: Libertarian Principles and Psychiatric Practices.* New Brunswick, NJ: Transaction, 2004.

———. *Fatal Freedom: The Ethics and Politics of Suicide.* 1999. Reprint, Syracuse: Syracuse Univ. Press, 2002.

———. *Ideology and Insanity: Essays on the Psychiatric Dehumanization of Man.* 1970. Reprint, Syracuse: Syracuse Univ. Press, 1991.

———. *Insanity: The Idea and Its Consequences.* 1987. Reprint, Syracuse: Syracuse Univ. Press, 1997.

———. *Law, Liberty, and Psychiatry: An Inquiry into the Social Uses of Psychiatry.* 1963. Reprint, Syracuse: Syracuse Univ. Press, 1989.

———. *Liberation by Oppression: A Comparative Study of Slavery and Psychiatry.* New Brunswick, NJ: Transaction, 2002.

———. *The Manufacture of Madness: A Comparative Study of the Inquisition and the Mental Health Movement.* 1970. Reprint, Syracuse: Syracuse Univ. Press, 1997.

———. *The Meaning of Mind: Language, Morality, and Neuroscience.* 1996. Reprint, Syracuse: Syracuse Univ. Press, 2002.

———. *The Myth of Mental Illness: Foundations of a Theory of Personal Conduct.* Rev. ed. 1961. Reprint, New York: HarperCollins, 2010.

———. *The Myth of Psychotherapy: Mental Healing as Religion, Rhetoric, and Repression.* 1978. Reprint, Syracuse: Syracuse Univ. Press, 1988.

———. *Our Right to Drugs: The Case for a Free Market.* 1992. Reprint, Syracuse: Syracuse Univ. Press, 1996.

———. *Pharmacracy: Medicine and Politics in America.* 2001. Reprint, Syracuse: Syracuse Univ. Press, 2003.

———. *Psychiatric Slavery: When Confinement and Coercion Masquerade as Cure.* New York: Free Press, 1977. Reprinted with a new preface as *Psychiatric Slavery.* Syracuse: Syracuse Univ. Press, 1998.

———. *Psychiatry: The Science of Lies.* Syracuse: Syracuse Univ. Press, 2008.

———. *Schizophrenia: The Sacred Symbol of Psychiatry.* 1976. Reprint, Syracuse: Syracuse Univ. Press, 1988.

———. *The Theology of Medicine: The Political-Philosophical Foundations of Medical Ethics.* 1977. Reprint, Syracuse: Syracuse Univ. Press, 1988.

Todd, J. *Mary Wollstonecraft: A Revolutionary Life.* New York: Columbia Univ. Press, 2000.

Tomalin, C. *The Life and Death of Mary Wollstonecraft.* New York: Harcourt Brace, 1974.

Vickers, H. *Alice: Princess Andrew of Greece.* New York: St. Martin's Press, 2000.

Waugh, A. *The House of Wittgenstein.* New York: Anchor Books, Random House, 2010.

Weaver, R. M. *Ideas Have Consequences.* Chicago: Univ. of Chicago Press, Phoenix Books, 1948.

Williams, T. *Memoirs.* 1975. Reprint, New York: Bantam, 1976.

Zweig, S. *Mental Healers: Franz Anton Mesmer, Mary Baker Eddy, Sigmund Freud.* Trans. E. Paul and C. Paul. 1931. Reprint, New York: Frederick Ungar, 1962.

Index

Acton, Lord, 57
Allen, Woody, 6
American Association for Emergency Psychiatry, 47–48
American Civil Liberties Union (ACLU), 53–54
American Foundation for Suicide Prevention (AFSP), 35–36, 84
American Psychiatric Association (APA), 17
Améry, Jean (Hans Maier), 62–65
Asclepius, 66
Assertive Community Treatment (ACT), 102–3
assisted suicide, 39–41. *See also* suicide
Atropos, 66
At the Mind's Limit (Améry), 64–65
Auden, W. H., 15
autohomicide, 8. *See also* suicide
autonomy, 78
Awl, William M., 70

Bayer, Ronald, 65
Bell, Luther V., 70
Bible, 3, 79
birth, 1
Bleuler, Eugen, 48–49

Bowker, Matthew, 42–43
Brown, Samuel, 82
Bynum, William F., 9

Camus, Albert, 13, 104
Carter, Zoe FitzGerald, 87–94
Centers for Disease Control and Prevention (CDC), 6
Chekhov, Anton, 27
Church of Euthanasia (CoE), 44
Clinton, Hillary, 74
Clinton, William J., 74
coerced drugging, 1, 12–13
coercion, psychiatric (civil commitment), 7–8. *See also* incarceration, psychiatric
contract: versus status, 17–19, 69–70

danger to self or others, xi–xii, 7–8. *See also* suicide
Declaration of Independence, 21
deinstitutionalization, 73–74
despotism, 20–21, 66–67
detention. *See* incarceration, psychiatric
determinism, 48–51, 57

diagnosis: not disease, 5, 7, 15
Dickenson, Donna, 99
Dignitas (Zurich), 39
DiLorenzo, Thomas J., 80
Dix, Dorothea Lynde, 71
Donaldson, Kenneth, 52–54

Eichmann, Adolf, 2
emergency psychiatry, 46–52
enumerated powers. *See* limited
    government
Epicurus, 6

"Federal Commitment to Suicide
    Prevention, The," 4–5
Frankl, Viktor Emil, 57–64
Freud, Sigmund, 15
From Death Camp to Existentialism
    (Frankl), 57
Fulford, K. W. M., 99

German–English: problems of trans-
    lation, 9
Goethe, Johann Wolfgang von, xi
Goin, Marcia, 17
good death, 87–94
Gore, Tipper, 89, 97

Hamlet (Shakespeare), 105
Health Resources and Services
    Administration (HRSA), 6, 66
Hemlock Society, 88–89
heterohomicide, 8. *See also* physi-
    cian-assisted suicide

Hippocrates, 6, 38
Hobson, Theo, 40–42
Holland, Julie, 46–47
Holocaust, 2
homosexuality, 37, 65, 99
Hume, David, xi, 64, 67, 109–11

Imperfect Endings (Carter), 87–94
incarceration, psychiatric, 43, 47,
    65–69, 78
Indian Health Service, 6, 66
insanitizing suicide, 11–12
Insanity: The Idea and Its Consequences
    (Szasz), 55

James, William, 48–49
Jefferson, Thomas, 20, 80–82

Kennedy, John F., 70, 74
Key, Francis Scott, 20
Kirkbride, Thomas S., 70
Korda, C., 44

Laing, R. D., 48
Langer, Lawrence, 60, 62
Laws (Plato), 95–96
liberty: mental patient's deprivation
    of, 7–8. *See also* incarceration,
    psychiatric
limited government, 21–22
Linde, Paul R., 47–48, 50–52, 54–55

Maine, Henry James Sumner, 18–19

malpractice: suicide as evidence of,
    ix–x
Mann, Horace, 70
Man's Search for Meaning (Frankl),
    59–62
McLean Asylum, 70
medical care: delivery of, 86–88
medicalization: of suicide, 9–12,
    88–89
medicine, 46
Mill, John Stuart, 12
Montaigne, Michel de, v
Moran, Mark, 83
Morrissey, Kevin, 56
Myth of Mental Illness, The (Szasz),
    54–5

national anthem (US), 20
National Institute of Mental Health
    (NIMH), 76
National Institutes of Health (NIH),
    6, 66
National Strategy for Suicide Pre-
    vention, 66
natural science, ix–x, 49–57
Neve, Michael, 9
Nietzsche, Friedrich, 9

O'Connor v. Donaldson (1974), 52–55
One Flew over the Cuckoo's Nest
    (Kesey), 55
"On Suicide" (Hume), xi, 81, 99–101
Ovid, 75

pediatric model: of psychiatry, 55

physician-assisted suicide, ix–x, 2.
    See also suicide
Pierce, Franklin, 70–73, 74
Plato, 95–96
power struggle: for medical privi-
    leges, 32
presidential letter of condolence, ix
primum non coercere (first, do not
    coerce), 97
primum non nocere (first, do no
    harm), 97
prohibition: contrasted with preven-
    tion, 13–15
psychiatric incarceration. *See* incar-
    ceration, psychiatric
Psychiatric Slavery (Szasz), 52
psychiatry, 16
psychoanalysis, 16
Pytell, T. E., 59, 61–62

Ratcliff, Mary Curtis, 87–94
Recollections (Frankl), 59
religion, 3, 78–80
Robespierre, M., 82
Romeo and Juliet (Shakespeare), 79
Royal Humane Society (RHS), 34–36
Rush, Benjamin, xi, 42

Schnipper, Steven, 37–39, 93
secrets, ix–x, 58–64
secularization, 7
Servatius, Robert, 2
Shelley, Mary (Mary Wollstonecraft
    Godwin), 33
Skorton, David J., 23–24
status. *See* contract

Substance Abuse and Mental
Health Services Administration
(SAMHSA), 6, 66
suicidality, xi. *See also* suicide
suicide: bombers, 75–76; emigration
as, 77–78, ideation, 8–9; insanitizing of, 11–12; Jefferson on, 80–82;
prevention contract, 17–18; rates,
4, 76; secession as, 80–82; taboo,
37–41; voluntary, 77–78; watch, 23
suicide prohibition measures:
Cornell University, 23–24; court
cases, 26–30; William and Mary
University, 24–25
Szasz, Thomas, 52, 54, 55

therapeutic state, 94, 104–5
Todd, Janet, 33–34
Torrey, E. Fuller, 102–3

US Constitution, 85
US Department of Health and
Human Services (HHS), 22, 66
Usenet, 84–86

Winerip, Michael, 37–39
Wollstonecraft Godwin, Mary
(Mary Shelley), 32–35
Woodhead, Chris, 39–40